Discovering Short Films

W0007548

Discovering Short Films

The History and Style of Live-Action Fiction Shorts

Cynthia Felando

palgrave
macmillan

DISCOVERING SHORT FILMS
Copyright © Cynthia Felando, 2015.

All rights reserved.

First published in 2015 by PALGRAVE MACMILLAN® in the United States—
a division of St. Martin's Press LLC, 175 Fifth Avenue, New York, NY 10010.

Where this book is distributed in the UK, Europe and the rest of the world,
this is by Palgrave Macmillan, a division of Macmillan Publishers Limited,
registered in England, company number 785998, of Houndmills, Basingstoke,
Hampshire RG21 6XS.

Palgrave Macmillan is the global academic imprint of the above companies
and has companies and representatives throughout the world.

Palgrave® and Macmillan® are registered trademarks in the United States, the
United Kingdom, Europe and other countries.

ISBN: 978-1-137-48847-3

Library of Congress Cataloging-in-Publication Data

Felando, Cynthia.
    Discovering short films : the history and style of live-action fiction shorts /
Cynthia Felando
        pages   cm
    Includes bibliographical references and index
    ISBN 978-1-137-48847-3 (alk. paper)
    1. Short films—History and criticism.   I. Title
    PN1995.F395 2015
    791.43'75—dc23   2015001266

A catalogue record of the book is available from the British Library.

Design by SPi Global.

First edition: July 2015

10 9 8 7 6 5 4 3 2 1

For Douglas

Contents

List of Figures

1

Introduction

In Spike Jonze's short musical/romantic-comedy/tragedy, *How They Get There* (1997), a young woman and man catch each other's gaze and proceed to flirt as they amble along opposite sides of a city street. The two seem destined for a happily ever after ending, at least until the unexpected occurs and the distracted young man steps into the path of a car. Then, in a sequence worthy of a high-budget action feature, he is struck and slams into the car's windshield as his shoe sails high into the air and lands alone in the gutter, thus answering the title's riddle, "how they get there." It all takes place in just over two minutes. *How They Get There* is a testament to the pleasures of the live-action fiction short film, including its meticulous narrative compression, preference for intense endings, and knack for flouting feature film conventions.

For short film cinephiles this is an enormously exciting time as shorts are more visible and easier to access than ever before. Certainly, the most profound recent development is the easier online availability of both old and new titles, which has elevated the fortunes of the short film so dramatically that film critics have declared we are in the midst of "a bonanza time"[1] and a period of "renaissance" and "rebirth."[2] Not surprisingly, a recent theme in mainstream film criticism concerns the growing popularity and cultural awareness of shorts, with many writers endorsing the artistry, creativity, and diversity of fiction shorts in particular. Several enthusiasts have celebrated the return of the short film to a position of prominence not enjoyed since the feature-length film began to supersede it in production, distribution, and exhibition in the mid-1910s. Quite simply, shorts are now the most available and likely most popular film form on the Internet. During a recent Academy Awards season, *The New York Times* reviewer A. O. Scott made a case for the worthiness of the short film in his review of the year's Oscar nominees: "In the past, opportunities to see the shorts were scarce, but lately they have been showing up in theaters and also on iTunes and cable. Their wider availability makes sense in an era that might well turn out to be a golden age of short-form moviemaking. The newer platforms favor brevity, and there is plenty of room for real cinema."[3]

Although film journalists have taken notice of the short film's higher profile in our media landscape and have celebrated the form in general, film and media studies scholars have not. The oversight is unfortunate, given the timeliness of the subject and the many possibilities for researching and appreciating it. Certainly, however, such opportunities also bring significant challenges. The most immediate is the persistent bias among scholars in favor of the feature-length film to the detriment of the short. This scholarly bias, not surprisingly, is echoed by the film industry's own marginalization of the short as less economically viable than the feature. Also, in short film research specifically, the focus tends to be upon animated and avant-garde shorts, so the scope and significance of live-action fiction titles are virtually unrecognized. To date, only two books in English focus on live-action fiction shorts from the studio era: Edwin M. Bradley's *The First Hollywood Sound Shorts, 1926–1931* and Leonard Maltin's *The Great Movie Shorts: Those Wonderful One- and Two-Reelers of the Thirties and Forties*. Both are excellent resources and have been instrumental in the historical survey in chapter two (herein). In addition, only one English-language monograph focuses specifically on the live-action fiction short in the post-studio era, Richard Raskin's *The Art of the Short Fiction Film: A Shot by Shot Study of Nine Modern Classics*. Raskin provides a useful category, the "modern short fiction film," which he argues is distinctive for combining "the originality of the experimental short with the telling of a coherent story."[4]

For Raskin, the first modern short fiction film is Roman Polanski's *Two Men and a Wardrobe* (1958). Using a case-study approach, starting with *Two Men*, Raskin focuses on seven additional shorts and one anthology film, all of which were made during a relatively brief period of time, between 1988 and 1997. In addition to brief analytical essays, there is a fascinating assortment of supplementary materials, including interviews with filmmakers, scripts, and storyboards for selected films. The author's enthusiasm for live-action fiction shorts is reflected in his curatorial focus on a smaller collection of titles and the scope of attention paid to the individual films, each of which has a running time of fifteen minutes or less.[5] *Discovering Short Films* aims to enlarge the discussion by addressing the ways in which the storytelling conventions and aesthetic practices of shorts differ from those of feature-length films and by considering a wider range of titles and running times.

Due to the paucity of published material, undertaking research in the area of live-action fiction shorts is daunting because the field lacks the canon that would likely develop in the wake of scholarly inquiry, and the sheer numbers of worthy titles from throughout film history are overwhelming. Without the foundation a canon provides, of course, one cannot presuppose a shared familiarity with a substantial or even limited body of work. Thus, as Janet Staiger observes, the efficiency of selecting films for and creating canons in order to enable knowledge among readers serves the "worthwhile goal of putting some order into the apparent chaos of so many films."[6] It certainly behooves the field of film and media studies to undertake the considerable yet necessary project of enabling the development of a short film canon. The enormity of the charge recalls the acknowledgment by legendary American film critic and auteur theorist Andrew Sarris regarding feature-length films of at least one hour in length that, given the quantity of titles from throughout film history, a systematic approach was necessary for organizing and categorizing them for cinephiles, critics, students, and scholars.[7] Toward that end, Sarris's aim was to provide specific recommendations for film enthusiasts by means of a sizable list of worthy films. Sarris's observations about the feature-length film are also germane to short film research and appreciation. That is, arguing in favor of a focus on individual films, he noted the prevailing tendency among critics to approach the Hollywood film industry as a monolith and to dismiss it, without regard to specific, often worthy, films. As he put it: "The trouble up to now has been not seeing the trees for the forest. But why should anyone look at thousands of trees if the forest itself be deemed aesthetically objectionable?"[8] Unfortunately, given the general marginalization of the short film among scholars and critics, there has been little attention to either the forest *or* the trees. This volume aims to direct attention to both.

During the 1960s and 1970s, when shorts of all kinds—live-action and animated, nonfiction and fiction—were widely distributed nontheatrically, especially in primary and secondary schools, several reference books were published that sought to tackle the problem posed by a general lack of knowledge about the films. The authors provided lists and synopses of recommended titles that educators could use for pedagogical purposes that ranged from enhancing students' general aesthetic and film appreciation to providing scientific knowledge and insights about important social issues (like teen drug use). In 1975, George Rehrauer addressed the lack of a short film canon and his effort to intervene by offering a long list of five hundred titles that he claimed were "regarded highly and recommended often" and that had "stood the tests of time, changing audiences, and different historical periods." He emphasized the difficulties involved due to the vast numbers of available titles: "The challenge to anyone compiling a list of short films for any purpose is enormous. To attempt a listing of the best films approaches the impossible."[9] More recently, the lack of a canon has been acknowledged by short film writers too, especially the authors of how-to books on filmmaking. Ric Beairsto, for example, refers to the issue as follows: "One of the chronic problems with short screenwriting texts is that it is virtually impossible for the author and reader to share a common reference base in short films. There just aren't enough of them around that we are collectively familiar with."[10] Unfortunately, the solution offered by some writers who purport to focus on shorts is to use feature-length films for their analytical models instead of shorts. Clifford Thurlow, for example, confesses: "Throughout the text, examples have been taken from features, not short films, simply because there are so few universally recognized short films to quote from."[11] The scholar Richard Raskin offers a more satisfying and useful though somewhat cumbersome remedy: for each of the individual shorts he analyzes in *The Art of the Short Fiction Film*, he includes a still image to illustrate each shot, which he calls "shot-by-shot reconstructions."[12]

The widespread neglect of live-action fiction shorts is demonstrated and perhaps exacerbated by the Library of Congress's National Film Registry, whose mandate is to officially recognize and ensure the preservation of American motion pictures of all kinds, from throughout film history, that have been deemed "national treasures." Unfortunately, the registry's shorts are mostly animated and avant-garde titles. Further, the few live-action fiction titles that have been added to the registry are mostly from the silent era; many significant later titles have been overlooked.[13] The registry's preferences are unsurprising, however, as they reflect the general lack of attention to the live-action fiction short, despite its longevity and significance throughout film history, as well as its prominence in our current media environment.

The general neglect of the short film is further suggested by the repetition of rhetorical questions posed by critics, such as "What's a Short Film, Really?" or "What Is Cinema—What Is Short Film?"[14] In 2004, the film journal *Sight and Sound* ran an article with the cheeky title "Eat My Shorts," which asked the provocative question: "What are short films for?" The answers speak to the enduring tension between artistic and commercial aims, and the piece ends with a decidedly downbeat suggestion:

> On the one hand, there's a tradition of artistic film-makers who see the short as an art form in its own right . . . On the other hand, the film industry and the media see shorts mostly as personal ads for would-be feature film-makers, an information flow to watch warily in case a director of stand-out talent . . . should show up. For everyone else, short films have been classed as of little importance.[15]

Sight and Sound's notions about the functions and merits of shorts for filmmakers and the industry are indicative of the general discourses about them; however, although live-action fiction short films in particular are mostly ignored among critics and scholars, the form does have several advocates and defenders. But it is also the case that many who tout the form's worthiness as art and entertainment often contribute further to its marginalization. To provide a sense of the general approaches to and conclusions about short films, it helps to examine the most prominent discourses about them, with attention to the many ways that writers both celebrate and arguably undermine them too. In addition, the efforts of writers to characterize and define the general category of the short film according to both running time and type will be examined. The discussion is intended to underscore the range of perspectives that characterize several published discourses about short films; primary documents consulted for this purpose include how-to literature for short filmmakers, as well as film reviews and commentary. Not surprisingly, the lack of attention to shorts in scholarship and criticism is not reflected in how-to discourses, as there are dozens of short filmmaking manuals currently in print, which are useful primary resources for assessing a variety of viewpoints about the short film. In general, although the manuals purport to endorse or otherwise favor the short film, it is also the case that they contribute to its marginalization, as the following discussion suggests.

Certainly, the marginalization of the short is nothing new. It began in the mid-1910s, during the period of the transition to the feature-length film as the preferred studio production strategy. Although the short film survived, it is nevertheless the case that today the live-action fiction short is generally characterized as a transitional form—as a useful practice medium for students or aspiring filmmakers, a way to demonstrate a filmmaker's readiness to move into feature-length filmmaking, and as the very rare theatrical prefeature screening. Manual writers typically frame their discussions in terms of the professional value shorts can provide to ambitious filmmakers, while ignoring their potential value as art and entertainment.

Specifically, they advise readers to make shorts in order to learn and develop their filmmaking skills, and to do so with an eye toward making something strong enough to serve as a portfolio piece. Beairsto's conclusion is fairly typical: "The short film is now mainly a form of apprenticeship."[16] Likewise, Bevin Yeatman argues that making shorts "is often a transitional stage, a game to pass beyond to the 'real' business of feature film."[17] Although Patrick Nash is more expansive about the advantages of the form as a learning medium, he shares the opinion that its ultimate value is to enable hopeful filmmakers to prepare for careers in features; as he explains: "Short film is an excellent training ground for writers and filmmakers alike. It's a place where you can experiment, develop and learn, make mistakes, acquire a broad range of filmmaking skills . . . and perfect your craft before trying to join the mainstream" of feature-length production.

But, by far, the most common observation about the value of short filmmaking concerns the short's usefulness as a "calling card" to demonstrate a filmmaker's talents to a film studio, producer, agent, or investor. One writer puts it simply: "The primary audience for the short film is the industry itself."[18] Similarly, Nash advises would-be feature filmmakers that their short film work "will be your calling card. It will help you to break into one of the most competitive industries on Earth."[19] Yet, at least one film critic has noted the significance of the historical shift implied by the calling card or "stepping stone" viewpoint as follows: "The evolution of the role of the short film is a fascinating journey from producing a work of art for its own creation to doing this as a means to a final, bigger end for new filmmakers."[20] The calling card perspective is so pervasive that the Telluride Film Festival offers a sidebar program of short films, "Calling Cards," that focuses on "Exceptional new works from promising filmmakers."[21] Without a doubt, demonstrating one's skills in shorts can be an effective way into a potentially productive career as a feature-length filmmaker, and for many established and even legendary filmmakers, the road to feature film success began with their shorts. Yet it's also the case that several, including Jim Jarmusch, Wes Anderson, and Spike Jonze, have continued to make shorts after establishing themselves as feature filmmakers. And, for his part, Jonze has said that he believes his short films have as much artistic merit as his feature-length films.[22] Noel McLaughlin, one of the few writers to object to the calling card angle, concludes that it's an approach that seriously limits the cultural value of shorts by reducing them to a subset of the feature-length film industry; as he argues: "Short filmmaking should not be seen as simply servicing the world of features but as a significant component of film culture in its own right."[23]

Interestingly, although the short film tends to be subservient to the feature-length film in the United States, several Western and Eastern European countries have a history of supporting and otherwise honoring the form. In terms of the contemporary shorts landscape, Pat Cooper and Ken Dancyger observe the difference as follows: "The short, at least in North America, is more and more an economic necessity for the student filmmaker and the novice professional . . . In Europe, however, the short film remains a viable form of expression, one supported in large part by cultural ministries. Magazines devoted to short films as well as festivals devoted exclusively to the form assure, at least for the medium term, that it will continue to thrive."[24] Not surprisingly perhaps, the highest profile shorts-only festivals are both in Europe: Clermont-Ferrand International Short Film Festival in France, and the International Short Film Festival Oberhausen in Germany. In addition, Shorts International Ltd.'s cable channel "ShortsTV" was launched in France and is now available throughout Europe (as well as in Middle Eastern and African countries). The company's founder, Carter Pilcher, claims there is a "much greater understanding of shorts in Europe . . . The reception is unbelievable. Everyone knows what a short film is, and is excited to be able to watch them."[25]

Nevertheless, those who consider shorts, in general or individually, as worthy of attention beyond their usefulness as a means to a professional end are rare. Individual shorts are seldom discussed on their own terms and merit as aesthetic, entertainment, and historical objects. It's also the case that writers who endorse the short film often make the case for its worthiness by means of comparisons to the feature-length film. One common argument is that shorts can be as and sometimes more compelling, complex, and pleasurable than features. Derrick Knight and Vincent Porter, for example, insist that equating the length of a film with depth is imprudent: "Brevity is too often mistaken for superficiality, spareness for triviality. The short can provide a welcome contrast to the long, heaving and ponderous super-film."[26] Also common are claims about the extra effort and talent required for short filmmaking, which often recall Henry David Thoreau's advice to a friend about story length, in which he acknowledged: "Not that the story need be long, but it will take a long while to make it short."[27] Susanne Reinker, for example, emphasizes the demands of crafting economical narratives and concludes that the short presents "the formidable artistic challenge of telling a story in the least possible time."[28] Clifford Thurlow agrees, saying "the script for a short film is more important and perhaps more difficult to write than a feature, simply because the brush strokes by necessity must be fine and detailed, each moment perfect."[29] Finally, making his case for the artistic virtues as well as challenges of the short film, A. O. Scott also uses the feature as a point of comparison: "A 10- or 15-minute movie requires as much craft and discipline as a feature. Maybe more. A short story can display infelicities of prose less forgivingly than a novel, and there is less room for error in a handful of shots and scenes. And a lot of room for artistry."[30] Using yet another strategy, some writers tout the short's greater creative possibilities and freedom— also relative to the feature-length film. Claims about the freedoms of short filmmaking often include an economic component, with the most common argument taking the position that because shorts are usually independent productions with smaller budgets relative to feature films, filmmakers can pursue bold artistic aims and riskier content. Legendary screenwriting teacher Richard Walter, for example, insists that: "In truth, the world of the short film—both creatively and commercially—holds far more possibilities for expression, to say nothing of production, than that of the feature."[31] William H. Phillips concurs: "A short fictional film is . . . a flexible and expressive form in its own right. Its brevity . . . can be an advantage . . . [A] short film may be more compressed, demanding, and subtle."[32] Knight and

Porter make the point most succinctly: "The possibilities for short film-making are endless."[33]

An apparent strength of the short film is that definitions of the form seem unnecessary. Running time is the essential feature. Yet, as short film discourses demonstrate, the issue is complicated both by the range of opinions about running times and by the variety of films often included in the general short film category. Film festivals, critics, scholars, and manual writers tend to disagree about the maximum running time that may be regarded as "short" but in general it ranges from fifteen to sixty minutes. Although pronouncements about maximum or preferred running times are not always, strictly speaking, oriented to defining the short film, they do function to characterize the form according to such preferences.

Film festivals and competitions set length limits for submissions that are considerably varied, from Cannes's fifteen-minute maximum to the Academy of Motion Picture Arts and Sciences's forty-minute maximum to the Los Angeles International Film Festival's sixty-minute limit. For their part, short filmmaking manuals tend to advocate shorter running times, and they offer a variety of reasons for their preferences. Favoring the commercial angle, Beairsto recommends running times of fifteen minutes or less, and suggests that filmmakers interested in longer shorts should consider exhibition opportunities by "produc[ing] a film that will constitute a commercial television half-hour."[34] For optimal festival consideration, Sundance programmer Roberta Munroe warns that shorts longer than twenty to thirty minutes are rarely invited because they limit the number of titles that can be included in individual shorts programs, and films chosen for prefeature screenings tend to be even shorter.[35] On storytelling grounds, Cooper and Dancyger prefer films of thirty minutes or less, arguing that longer running times "usually need a secondary, or minor, plot-line" to warrant their length.[36] Perhaps the most atypical rationale for shorter running times is short film scholar Raskin's; limiting his analyses to titles of fifteen minutes or less, he claims the viewer's experience is the key consideration: "The density of the storytelling found in the true short fiction film . . . engages the viewer's concentration in a way that cannot be sustained beyond about 15 minutes."[37]

The short film's fairly wide range of running times has prompted writers to propose terminology that conveys finer distinctions. As Andrew Lund explains, "Let's say shorts run anywhere from 5 to 40 minutes . . . a spread of 400%—that's quite a lot of territory for the 'short' to cover. The short designation should really be divided into more precise categories."[38] Although relatively rare, a few platforms do observe such distinctions. At the shorter end, for example, some shorts-dedicated websites designate "short shorts" and "micro shorts" as films that run five minutes or less.[39] At the longer end, as Raskin notes, in some locations shorts with twenty-to-forty-minute running times have their own designations; for example, they are called "novellefilms" in Scandinavian countries and "moyen metrage" in France. The term "novellefilm" is borrowed from the short story realm; that is, the German term "novelle" specifies medium-length fiction narratives, while the French term "nouvelle" refers to a story longer than twenty pages, which falls between the short story and the novel.[40]

In addition to running time, discourses often address the types of films that can be included in the general short film category. Besides the most common categories of fiction and nonfiction, animated and live-action, narrative and experimental, writers have offered long lists of possibilities that include a variety of industrial, commercial, student, and professional categories. R. W. Wolf, for example, provides a rather unwieldy selection: "both black-and-white and hand-coloured films, documentaries, fiction, experimental films, animation, dramas and melodramas, thrillers and horror films, slapstick and comedy, as well as commercials, cultural and education films and artists' films."[41] Symon Quy also favors an inclusive approach, asserting that the short's flexibility is "perhaps its greatest asset; it crosses the boundaries of all categories of film production."[42] Arguably, however, including so many different kinds of filmmaking practice, many of which are also relevant to feature-length films, complicates the development of systematic critical and analytical methods that are germane to each or all of the categories. Indeed, the scholarly neglect of shorts may reflect the tendency to include such disparate practices in the general category, thus making it unproductive and, perhaps, meaningless. Although live-action fiction shorts are virtually unknown to film and media studies, in terms of a larger cultural awareness, their wider availability has reinvigorated the form's visibility and popularity. The pleasures and possibilities of the live-action fiction short are immense, as are the many levels of inquiry and appreciation that can be brought to this timely and worthy new field of study. As this volume demonstrates, live-action fiction shorts have considerable artistic, narrative, and historical value. Not only do they vastly outnumber feature-length films, they can inform a richer understanding both of film history and our current shorts-saturated landscape. For these reasons, and also because shorts are indicators of old and new trends, styles, filmmakers, and national cinemas, they deserve serious attention by film and media scholars. To address the many gaps in our knowledge about the fiction short, *Discovering Short Films* provides a survey of its history from the silent era to the present, an understanding of its characteristic storytelling strategies, and categories for organization and analysis.

The general category of the live-action fiction short is defined very simply: it refers to films of any length up to sixty minutes. In addition, titles are organized according to two broad categories: the classical short and the art short. The terms "classical" and "art" are strategic and benefit from film and media scholars' familiarity with the concepts as they relate to the feature-length film. In the most general terms, both categories are characterized by the short film's preference for simple stories without subplots that focus on a single event or situation during a brief story time. In addition, both categories reflect the diversity of the feature-length film realm, with content that ranges from sentimental to raw and visual strategies that range from naturalistic to highly stylized. Arguably, however, the parameters of the short film are much wider than for the feature-length film and enable a greater variety of offbeat, bold, and entertaining content and style. To convey the development, diversity, and richness of the form, *Discovering Short Films* considers national and international titles from throughout film history, including landmark and better-known shorts, as well as several lesser-known yet noteworthy titles. In addition, there is attention to shorts with a range of running times—from "short shorts" of five minutes or less, to longer ones of more than thirty minutes, and with a range of complexity, from very spare narratives to those with more elaborate plots that, like the classical Hollywood feature, use the occasional subplot.

As the following discussions and analyses suggest, a particular strength and pleasure of the short film is that its narratives are often elliptical and tend to favor the focus on moments or "fragments" of time. The form's attention to relatively contained periods of time precludes the narrative "arc" and character development familiar in the feature-length film, so there are few heroes and love stories in the short. Furthermore, given the youth of many short filmmakers, it is unsurprising that the focus on youth-oriented content is common in the fiction short and is reflected in the preponderance of young protagonists, coming-of-age narratives, and vignettes or slice-of-life depictions of youth. Such shorts tend to tap into universal themes regarding the significance of youth and its challenges and occasionally its triumphs, so they travel well and are as familiar in international titles as in those from the United States. In addition, the spare or entirely dialogue-free film is one of the most consistent and persistent strategies in the short film; although nearly unknown in today's feature-length films, it's a significant legacy of the silent era and the strategy provides several benefits, including the ability to cross language barriers and to work in the service of narrative economy and brisk pacing.

Although they fall outside the scope of this survey, omnibus and anthology films, which are feature-length films that consist of several short works or "episodes," are tangentially related to the live-action fiction short and are therefore worth addressing briefly. Historically important categories, omnibus and anthology collections were often prestige productions during Hollywood's classical era because they enabled studios to capitalize on their production and talent resources by featuring well-known directors and stars. They were also popular in Europe during the 1950s and 1960s, especially among New Wave directors. Nevertheless, like short films, both omnibus and anthology films are underappreciated by film scholars. As a result, David Scott Diffrient's recent monograph, *Omnibus Films: Theorizing Transauthorial Cinema*, provides a welcome addition to the larger discussion of shorts. Distinguishing between "omnibus films," which have two or more directors (such as *Quartet* [1948]), and "anthology films," which have one director (such as Jim Jarmusch's *Coffee and Cigarettes* [2003]), Diffrient does not refer to their individual entries as "shorts," but rather as "episodes." Further, he defines the episode as "*an individual, coherent story, vignette, or sustained narrative event in itself.*"[43] Making a strong case for characterizing the omnibus film as a single feature that consists of several short episodes, Diffrient underscores the significance of the connections between the individual parts and the larger whole, which he refers to as the "miniature/gigantic dialectic."[44] Accordingly, he conceptualizes the omnibus film as one that is "subject to a kind of textual flux and inter-episodic flow which result from several author-directors' segments being combined as autonomous yet connected units in a *single motion picture.*"[45] Specifically, Diffrient argues that the separate episodes that constitute an omnibus or anthology film "should not be analyzed in isolation, individually, as autonomous short films shorn from their narrative 'housing.'"[46] Certainly, there might also be a case to be made for considering certain omnibus episodes separately. Indeed, although the impulse will be resisted in the present volume, in some cases a single episode stands out so singularly in an omnibus or anthology collection that it begs individual attention, as with "14e Arrondissement," Alexander Payne's superb contribution to *Paris, Je T'Aime/Paris, I Love You* (2007), among many others.

As for the live-action fiction short, the research paths and possibilities for scholarly inquiry are both far-reaching and fascinating, and there are many rewards involved in their exploration, not the least of which is the continuation of recent efforts to rethink film and media scholarship by examining noncanonical forms and texts. In addition to Diffrient's monograph, the effort is well represented by *Learning with the Lights Off: Educational Film in the United States,* which considers the largely overlooked history of educational films, the majority of which, it is also worth noting, are shorts.[47] Certainly, the greater availability of shorts today enables scholars to reevaluate the feature-length film's dominance in critical and academic discourses. In addition, knowing more about shorts and their storytelling and visual practices also deepens our understanding of the feature-length film. Given the larger cultural awareness of short films today, there is an even greater urgency to the need for scholarly attention. Accordingly, *Discovering Short Films* aims to intervene decisively in this moment by calling attention to and enabling analyses of the vast universe of forgotten and overlooked live-action fiction shorts and by demonstrating their contributions to filmmaking and film history. The goals herein are ambitious: to rescue the live-action fiction short from critical and historical oblivion, to remove it from the margins, and to nourish its appreciation. Indeed, in film and media studies, we would do well to heed Virginia Woolf's advice: "Let us not take it for granted that life exists more in what is commonly thought big than in what is commonly thought small."[48]

Discovering Short Films is organized as follows: chapter two provides a survey of the short film's history from the silent era to the present, with primary attention to the United States, and argues that the short's history begins not with the "birth" of motion pictures but in the mid-1910s, during the rise of the feature-length film when the industry sought to distinguish the feature from what it called the "short subject." The chapter also considers several historical issues related to the production and exhibition of shorts, including the studio era's short film production units, the impact of the forced end of vertical integration and the demise of the studio system, and the post-studio era proliferation of film schools and courses. Chapter three makes a case for the specificities of the short fiction film and distinguishes it from the feature-length film based on their different storytelling strategies. Several elements that are specific to or most consistently found in fiction shorts are examined, including those related to unity, character and characterization, and endings. Chapter four addresses the storytelling conventions of the "classical short," which tends to be more highly plotted and to have more easily discerned meanings, familiar character types, linear organization, and closed endings. The chapter also considers the different strategies used in shorter shorts versus longer ones. Chapter five focuses on a conspicuous expansion of the fiction short's repertoire of storytelling and formal strategies, beginning in the mid- to late 1950s, with the emergence of the "art short." The development and greater diversity of the art short relative to the classical short is demonstrated by means of the analyses of several significant titles.

It should be noted that the film analyses in the following chapters are intended to enable familiarity with a substantial body of films and to provide a foundation that can serve as a jumping-off point for further research. However, it should also be noted that this survey is dependent upon the availability of titles and is not intended to be representative of the shorts of individual directors, national cinemas, eras, or genres. Rather it is meant to provide a first step that will enable finer distinctions and approaches. At present, the live-action fiction short canon is a small one that tends to favor silent era titles, so the discussion and analyses of titles from the classical to the contemporary era aims to provide some much-needed balance. Furthermore, a number of titles from well-known directors are discussed. Although a common approach among critics and scholars is to note the ways in which the early shorts of noteworthy filmmakers convey their subsequent auteur themes and preoccupations, which suggests their value primarily as precursors to the implicitly favored feature-length works, *Discovering Short Films* does not discuss individual titles in such terms. Finally, in the attempt to do justice to the live-action fiction short, it is nonetheless the case that time and space constraints mean that many, many worthy shorts cannot be discussed in the main text. As a result, the appendix provides summaries of titles that are historically and/ or aesthetically significant in order to encourage a more full-bodied appreciation and understanding of the live-action fiction short. This project takes great inspiration from Andrew Sarris's efforts to organize and recommend titles from among the thousands produced throughout film history to enable critical attention and to "establish a system of priorities for the film student"; as he observed, a systematic approach facilitates greater precision and analytical distinctions: "Comprehension becomes a function of comprehensiveness. As more movies are seen, more cross-references are assembled."[49] The nearly eighty entries listed in the appendix only scratch the surface of possibilities but are intended to be a step in the direction of comprehensiveness. The ultimate goal is to be inclusive regarding the live-action fiction shorts chosen for discussion, in the hope that it will inspire much additional attention. Of course, it is also hoped that readers will become viewers of the shorts discussed herein and that critics, filmmakers, students, and scholars will be inspired to undertake their own journeys of discovery.

2

Shorts and Film History:
The Rise, Fall, and Rise
of the Short Film

The history of the short film has been a tumultuous one, especially in comparison to the feature-length film. After a position of dominance in the earliest years of the developing studio system, the short was displaced by the feature and has remained a marginal player ever since. The shifts in the live-action fiction short's fortunes, in particular, are compelling and enable a fuller understanding of American film history during the studio and post-studio eras. In a history that parallels that of the feature-length film, the short has enjoyed many triumphs and landmarks that are evidenced by a remarkable legacy of films. This chapter surveys some of the most significant developments in the history of the short, from the silent era to the present and primarily in the United States. Beginning with the period of the form's marginalization when feature-length films became the dominant studio form, in the mid-1910s, the short's history is marked by some significant high points, including the flourishing of production in the early sound era and the enormously expanded storytelling and aesthetic strategies of the post-studio era. Today, the short film not only survives but, given the proliferation of screening platforms especially favorable to the form, the balance soon may tip in its favor, if it hasn't already. Following the general contours of American film history, this survey is oriented to putting shorts into that larger context and relies in large part upon excellent existing research. The aim is to provide a fairly contained account of a long period, and one that suggests the many possibilities available for further research and exploration.

The Rise of the Feature, the Fall of the Short

In discussions of the short film, the observation that the birth of motion pictures corresponds with the birth of the short film is almost ubiquitous. Indeed, as nearly every book and essay written about short films observes, "In the beginning, all films were short."[1] Arguably, however, a more precise and useful approach is to consider the short film's history as one that begins during the early-to-mid 1910s when the film industry sought to distinguish the developing feature-length film from the "short subject." As Patrick Nash notes, it was the emergence and development of the feature-length film that prompted the use of the term "short" in order to distinguish one-reel and two-reel films from multi-reel "features": "They came to be known as 'short films' or 'short subjects' as opposed to the longer 'feature films', and so the term 'short film' was born."[2]

The transition to the feature-length film as the industry standard took place between 1910 and 1915. As Janet Staiger notes, during that time films went from an average of eighteen minutes to seventy-five minutes and more in duration.[3] Not surprisingly, the shift to feature-length films included the industry's efforts to characterize them as higher quality relative to one-reel and two-reel films. Although quality had long been associated with films labeled as "features," it was not until the 1910s that the term designated a longer-duration film—of five reels or more. That is, in the early silent era, the term referred to films that warranted special treatment by being *featured* in advertising.[4] As the industry sought to elevate longer-duration films by referencing notions of "quality," rhetorical appeals emphasized the point by using comparative terms that explicitly or implicitly referred to one-reel films. Industry claims, for example, included that the multi-reel film was "a quality product" that offered something "better and bigger," "more effective," and "extra and of more importance" than the "shorter one-reel affair." Adding another rhetorical layer to the mix, the trade press appealed to theater owners by claiming the feature attracted higher quality patrons too, by drawing "the quicker-minded audience" and making a "deeper impression upon the memory," which provided greater advertising and profit possibilities than shorter films.[5]

In addition to equating the multi-reel film with higher quality, the differentiation of the feature from the short went further as the trade press and other industry discourses increasingly touted longer-duration, higher-budget films as unique, as individualized products—unlike the one-reel and two-reel films that were considered interchangeable parts of a standardized program and were not billed or advertised individually.[6] In a set of clever rhetorical moves, quality became a characteristic associated with the feature-length film almost exclusively. The issue was also relevant on several levels, from production to exhibition, as industry discourses cited everything from the bigger budgets, higher production values, and the greater narrative complexity of features, to their often more prestigious screening venues such as opera houses and legitimate theaters. Appeals to quality were made on the basis of class level too; inasmuch as feature-length films carried higher ticket prices, they were expected to attract higher-income, especially middle-class, audiences with more available leisure time and cash.[7] Certainly, the elevation of the feature-length film using the rhetoric of quality functioned to diminish, if not to disparage, the short film, and the term itself acquired several negative and enduring connotations, which only recently have begun to wane.

Late 1910s and 1920s

Of course, the short film survived the rise of the feature-length film. Production of live-action fiction shorts, especially comedies, continued. Certainly, one of the better-known aspects of short film history is that the biggest comic stars of the silent era, including Buster Keaton, Charlie

Chaplin, and Fatty Arbuckle, continued to make comedy shorts for several years, and they continued to enjoy enormous popularity. In addition, in the late 1910s and throughout the 1920s, several independent producers remained devoted to the production of comedy shorts, including Max Fleischer, Mack Sennett, and Hal Roach. As Kristin Thompson and Edwin Bradley both have noted, before the sound film revolution in the mid-1920s, the majority of fiction shorts were slapstick or "knockabout" comedies.[8] Dramatic shorts were much less common, but included Universal's two-reel "Mustang" Westerns series.[9]

In exhibition, shorts of varied lengths and types preceded the feature-length film as part of a standardized theatrical program by the mid-1910s; but, as Leonard Maltin has noted, theater owners often used the generic phrase "also selected short subjects" without specifying individual film titles in their advertisements.[10] As a result, moviegoers "came to expect one feature, a couple of shorts (which lasted from ten to twenty minutes), a newsreel, and possibly a stage show" in a theatrical program.[11] In the fiction short category specifically, the majority of theaters offered a one-reel or two-reel comedy as part of the pre-feature program.[12] For such programs, the feature-length film was the "main attraction," and the shorts were deemed supplemental and thus billed as "added" or "extra attractions," a status reflected in the perhaps unfortunate characterization of them as "fillers."[13] Nevertheless, despite their diminished status relative to the feature, shorts remained crucial to theater owners who wanted to present a "balanced" and varied program that would provide something of interest to everyone—in other words, for audiences characterized by different ages, genders, class levels, and interests.[14] As a result, until the end of the studio system, shorts were a significant part of each studio's output and profits, from production, to distribution, and exhibition. In addition, as several observers noted, their marginalization accorded shorts a certain freedom too. As Leonard Maltin explains:

> To the studios, they were part of the regular production schedule, usually quite profitable and therefore worthy of decent budgets and a

fair amount of publicity. But at the same time, shorts were only shorts, and the studio executives let the specialists in charge of their production work as an autonomous unit, without interference. As long as the product came out on time, was fairly well received, and turned a profit, there was no need to get involved as they would in feature-film production.[15]

Shorts and the Sound Revolution

For the most part, film historians have addressed the subject of shorts in the 1920s in relation to their part in the technological innovation and development of sound production strategies. As many have noted, when synchronous sound films were introduced to audiences, it happened by way of short films. There has been particular attention to the importance of Warner Bros. as a leader in the motion picture sound revolution with its sound-on-disc shorts. But, as Donald Crafton points out, in the earliest days of synchronous sound, "'sound film' usually meant music, not speech."[16] Warners quickly seized the lead in sound shorts production with its enormously popular Vitaphone musicals that featured Broadway and vaudeville performers, which soon inspired other studios to follow their lead.[17] With the success of the musical shorts, the studios expanded their output by producing talking shorts too, mostly comedies, in which well-known stage and radio personalities, like Eddie Cantor, perform their presentation-style comedy routines. As for fiction shorts with dialogue, by 1928 Warners had added "Vitaphone Playlets" to its production schedule. The Playlets, usually about twenty-minutes long, are dialogue-based adaptations of theatrical productions with content that ranges from serious drama to, much more frequently, comedies. One of the most important developments of the early silent era was that sound "opened up a new world of verbal comedy" for short films, and dialogue-based comedies were soon considered superior to their slapstick counterparts.[18] As Maltin and Rob King note, two primary kinds of comedy are represented in the studio era short; in Maltin's terminology, they are "either slapstick or situation comedy"; for King, the two strains are dialogue based, which was considered sophisticated, versus slapstick, which was disparaged as crude. Indeed, in terms of the prevailing viewpoint about shorts during the early sound period, even in the context of a form that had long been positioned lower on the hierarchy of commercial film production, the disregard for the early sound shorts—especially comedies—was particularly strong.[19]

The early dialogue-based shorts are set bound, often frontally arranged sketches with long-duration wide shots that mimic live stage performances. The Vitaphone "Varieties" shorts are noteworthy both because they were stand-alone comedies and dramas, and they suggest the range of content of the early sound era. A large proportion of the earliest Varieties are comedy skits or dialogues performed vaudeville style with frontal staging by well-known acts; however, there are several more plot-oriented titles, including those that use a few separate scenes and locations. Several of the plot-driven Varieties titles were directed by Bryan Foy, which are distinctive for a simple yet slightly more dynamic visual style dependent upon varied camera angles and distances. Interestingly, the Varieties shorts also suggest that studio era shorts tended to resist love stories, as both the dramas and comedies include titles that feature gently bickering couples, suffering wives and abusive or philandering husbands, or happy couples in the midst of setbacks. A common scenario in the comedy shorts concerns husbands doing their best to stay away from their wives, to go out with their buddies, or to make time with other women. The 1929 single-reel Varieties title *Surprise* (Foy) is a typically silly marriage comedy in which a husband who's a cheat, or would-be cheat, is lured by his friend to a surprise party with the promise that he'll meet two attractive young women. When the husband arrives, he laments that the guests all know him so he'll be unable to enjoy an interlude with one of the young women. The husband's goose is cooked when one of the party guests informs his wife about his whereabouts, and she arrives to discover him flirting with a young woman, to which she responds by fighting him Punch-and-Judy style before snatching him away from the party. It ends a few days later when the husband runs into the friend who's got another couple of girls lined up, but the morose husband can't get away because he's bound to his wife—with handcuffs.

As for early dialogue-based dramatic shorts, although they were produced less often than comedies, there are several noteworthy titles that reflect Bradley's observation that by 1930 and 1931 there was "less of the vaudeville influence and more of the so-called real world" in shorts.[20] Further, as the next examples suggest, during the studio era of short film production, when the aim was to appeal to and entertain general audiences, the focus was upon easy-to-follow stories and recognizable character types with understandable motivations and goals in both short comedies and dramas. Often the "real world" was represented in shorts that depicted slice-of-life narratives that were oriented to depicting the hardships of family life, especially those that were understandable in the context of the Great Depression. Warners's shorts in particular explored challenging material in their attention to gritty subjects and the disillusionment of protagonists. Certainly, Warners is well known for its social issues–oriented feature-length films, such as Mervyn LeRoy's *I Am a Fugitive from a Chain Gang* (1932), but the presence of such content in short films is especially remarkable given the emphasis on comedy in studio era shorts.

The Hard Guy (Hurley, 1930) features Spencer Tracy in an early film role and provides a strong example of a powerful yet simple narrative that addressed the era's economic challenges and conveys the dramatic intensity that at least a few producers brought to fiction shorts in the early sound era. Despite its short six-minute running time, *The Hard Guy* is remarkable for its gritty story of a young family caught in the net of the Depression, if not for its low-budget set and sometimes awkward cinematography. Following a slang-filled monologue about the impossibility of finding a job and providing the necessary care for their sick little girl, the young "hard guy" husband—a decorated war veteran—recounts a news story about the arrest of a poor "sap" caught trying to steal money for his kids after unsuccessfully "pounding the pavement" for a year. As the husband predicts, the sap will "pound rock for the next ten." Tension builds when the husband leaves to look for work, with his gun in his pocket, while his fretful wife waits (see Figure 2.1). Following the sounds of a street shooting just outside, apparently between a robber and the cops,

Figure 2.1 *The Hard Guy* (1930)

the husband returns with a pile of food and a doll for his daughter. But, the happy ending reveals a twist: the husband has not robbed anyone, as his wife feared, but instead he's sold his military-issue gun to buy everything legally.

Niagara Falls (McGann) is a Vitaphone Varieties short from 1930 that offers a more sentimental portrait of a happily married couple who remain resolute in their love despite a recurring setback. *Falls* opens with a new young wife happily preparing for her Niagara Falls honeymoon when she gets a call from her mother with news about her father's financial distress. The couple agrees to help by forfeiting their honeymoon cash, but they promise each other they'll soon enjoy a delayed honeymoon. Five years later, the couple is packing again for their trip to the Falls when their little boy gets sick, which delays their journey once again. Twenty-five years later, the now-elderly couple is looking forward to their long-awaited trip, when the police arrive to announce that their adult son has absconded with five hundred dollars from the bank that employs him, which is the precise sum the couple has saved for their honeymoon. To protect their son, the wife and husband agree once again to forfeit their trip by paying the bank. The film ends with the sad but still loving couple gazing upon a calendar photograph of the Falls after the husband has turned on the water taps to give the sensation that they're actually there. Although the couple has an enduring marriage, *Niagara Falls* shares the convention of many fiction shorts to resist a happily ever after ending.

Trifles (Foy) is an even harder-edged Vitaphone Varieties short from 1930. A largely faithful adaptation of the well-known one-act play from 1915 by Susan Glaspell, *Trifles* is also one of the strongest of the early sound era studio shorts. A morality tale, it opens with a farm wife, Mrs. Wright, tending to her beloved singing canary, when her husband storms into the room angry about the bird's "squawking." As he aggressively approaches the cage, the wife cries out and the scene ends. In the next scene, when a neighboring farmer arrives and asks to meet with her husband, the wife sits, apparently dazed, and responds that her husband is unavailable because he's been hanged in his sleep—but she doesn't know who killed him. In the third and final scene, the farmer and his wife, the sheriff and his wife, and the county prosecutor have arrived in order for the men to complete their investigation of the husband's death and for the women to collect some things for Mrs. Wright, whom we learn has been detained as a suspect. The sheriff and prosecutor are both condescending about the wife's housekeeping and they mock the women when they overhear them discussing the farm wife's quilting project; nevertheless, the men ask the women to share anything that might be helpful in the investigation, especially anything that might suggest a motivation for the murder. While the men are out of the kitchen (the only setting), the two women discover the empty ruined cage and the dead canary in a little box, and they realize that the husband killed the bird, despite the fact that it was perhaps the only bright spot in his wife's lonely life. Mrs. Wright's heartbroken neighbor regrets that "I might have known she needed help. I know how things can be for a woman." When the sheriff's wife recounts a horrible childhood event when a boy killed her kitten with an axe, she confesses her temporarily violent intentions.

In the end, the two women hide the evidence to protect Mrs. Wright, and the ironic meaning of the title is revealed: when the insensitive sheriff scoffs at the absurdity of the accused wife's worries about inconsequential domestic affairs while she's suspected of murder, the neighboring farmer agrees, saying, "Well, women are used to worrying over trifles." Even in the context of the Depression, *Trifles* is a remarkably feminist film about women's solidarity and wisdom. In addition, for a short film especially, *Trifles*' open ending is unconventional because, although it answers the question regarding the women's decision to withhold their evidence about Mrs. Wright's potential motivation for breaking her husband's neck, it does not answer the question regarding what her future will be. Arguably, the provocative content and interpretive latitude enabled by *Trifles* mark it as a significant precursor to the art shorts that were made in the post-studio era of the 1950s and beyond.

Shorts and the Studio Era

As the studios consolidated their power in the late 1920s, in part, by developing standardized products, shorts were a significant part of their efforts.[21] As King explains, "The film industry's structure as a mature oligopoly, beginning in the early sound era, was secured in part through the majors' involvement in short subject production. The move by the major studios into the production of in-house short subjects during the mid-1920s . . . represented a fundamental step in their quest to dominate the film industry." By both producing and distributing shorts, the studios expanded their profits and position relative to independent shorts producers because they could provide theaters with a "full service" program of shorts and feature-length films. Short film production provided another benefit too, as it enabled the studios to enlarge their system of block-booking, in a practice called "full-line forcing," which required theater owners to accept complete packages that included shorts as well as features.[22]

The early sound period was a boom time for shorts because the studios and independent producers were committed to sound shorts before they moved into sound feature production. At the same time, theater owners increasingly substituted live acts and music with less expensive shorts. As a result, as Crafton notes, "The silent short subject disappeared much faster than the silent feature."[23] In terms of fiction shorts specifically, one of the most noteworthy aspects of the era is that titles were rarely free-standing, or one-off productions. Instead, the overwhelming majority of fiction shorts were series based, with continuity from episode to episode in terms of characters, performers, and situations. Bradley emphasizes the link between early sound era series shorts and their silent predecessors: "By 1931, the personality of the American short subject had undergone a second transformation from what it became during the first giddy months of sound . . . As they had before sound arrived, series were claiming a majority percentage of the Hollywood shorts output."[24] Moreover, it was comedies that dominated series shorts production in the early sound era as they did throughout the studio era.

The importance of series comedies is suggested both by their popularity and longevity. Among many others, Warners's popular Joe McDoakes "So You Want to . . ." comedy series featured an "average man" protagonist demonstrating the many possible and usually absurd travails and opportunities involved in various activities, from self-improvement schemes to personal and professional pursuits. Produced between 1942 and 1956, the titles of the series' sixty-three one-reel shorts (directed by Richard L. Bare) indicate their particular focus, including *So You Want to Give Up Smoking* (1942), *So You Want to Be in Pictures* (1947), and a clever parody of hard-boiled movie detectives, *So You Want to Be a Detective* (1948). MGM's biggest in-house series was the "Pete Smith Specialties," which included fiction and documentary comedies produced between 1934 and 1955.[25] At Columbia, *The Three Stooges* comedy series, produced between 1934 and 1959, was especially popular and profitable.[26]

Not surprisingly, given the success of the early sound shorts, in 1926 the trade paper *Variety* inaugurated a series of reviews called "Short Films."[27] In 1932, short films got another boost in recognition when the Academy of Motion Picture Arts and Sciences inaugurated

two short film awards, the first of which demonstrates the enduring prominence of comedy in shorts: "Short Subjects, comedy" and
"Short Subjects, novelty."

In 1936, a special issue of *Film Daily* focused on short subjects
and included the article, "Short Subjects Developing Ground for New
Talent Needed by Studios," written by Fred Quimby, then in charge
of MGM's shorts unit. Quimby touted the usefulness of shorts for
providing a "proving ground for new players," and cited the actor
Robert Taylor as one of the studio's successes: "In the short space of
a few months since he made his original screen appearance in the
first of the Crime Doesn't Pay series, Taylor has become one of the
screen's most popular leading men."[28] During the studio era, short
films were friendly to performers and filmmakers on the way up the
career ladder as well as those on the way down. The major studios
not only maintained shorts departments to supply their theaters with
a full program of films, the units also enabled the training and test-
ing of new filmmakers and performers. Paramount, for example, routinely recruited stars from Broadway and vaudeville for shorts, which
enabled the studio to gauge their potential popularity before signing
them to long-term contracts and feature-length films. For filmmakers
and performers whose greatest career success was behind them, a few
found a home, if only temporarily, in short films. The many future
stars that started in shorts include performers Frank Sinatra, Shirley
Temple, Danny Kaye, and Judy Garland, and directors such as Joseph
Losey, Don Siegel, and Jules Dassin. Those whose stars were dimming
that found work in shorts include Buster Keaton, Harry Langdon, and
Mack Sennett, all of whom worked for the low-prestige Educational
Pictures studio in the 1930s.[29]

Of course, there were filmmakers and performers who began in
shorts and remained there or continued to work there occasionally.
At least a few acknowledged their lower status relative to their feature-
length film colleagues, even when their short films were appreciated
by and popular among audiences and critics. Gertrude Astor, a working actress with the Hal Roach studio, acknowledged that appearing
in short comedies was "looked down upon" by others in the industry.

Likewise, Columbia director Edward Bernds recalled the disappointment of never being on the receiving end of commendations from the studio's brass: "We, the short subjects people, were ignored by the [studio] hierarchy. We were even separated from the main lot, housed in a shabby old building. . . . The lack of recognition . . . bothered me too. We'd make some films; perhaps we'd hit a hot streak . . . We knew the shows were good, but the [studio] bosses never bothered to look at our stuff."[30] However, although shorts continued to be considered a less prestigious form, until the dismantling of the studio system they had a significant place in production, distribution, and exhibition—with some serious setbacks and changes along the way. As Bradley notes, "The short subject would be a staple in the movie theater program for a generation . . . but its general importance would not be the same after the first few years of sound."[31] The reason: the double-feature program.

In the early years of the Depression, many theater owners began to offer double-feature programs in an effort to boost ticket sales. As a result, the programming strategy in which a collection of short films preceded a single feature-length film became much less common. So, with fewer program spots and less program time devoted to shorts, the studios not only reduced the numbers of shorts they produced, they also began to favor one-reel over two-reel shorts. By 1934, the major studios had moved to entirely cut or to seriously reduce their production of two-reel shorts.[32] The studios' preference for one-reel shorts is suggested by the announcement from the head of Paramount's Short Subject Department in 1936 that the studio would produce 112 single-reel shorts but only one two-reeler—a cartoon.[33]

The Demise of Studio Shorts

Several factors contributed to the demise of the studio-based short film units, starting in the late 1940s, including the end of vertical integration, competition from television, and vastly reduced box office profits. The most significant setback for short films occurred in 1948, when the US Supreme Court issued its landmark Paramount decree, which concluded that the major film studios had violated antitrust laws because they not only produced films, they distributed them, and most exhibited them in their extensive theater chains. The decree forced the majors to end their practices of vertical integration and marked the beginning of the end of the studio system. As a result, the studios began to liquidate their least profitable operations: their theater chains. The effects on short filmmaking and exhibition were immense as the studios at first dramatically reduced the numbers of shorts (and features) they produced and, by the late 1950s, discontinued the production of in-house live-action fiction shorts.[34] Columbia, for example, despite that it had long relied upon the profits and popularity of its shorts, ended its series production in 1956 and shuttered its shorts unit entirely in 1959. Likewise, Warner Bros. stopped producing live-action shorts in 1956 (though the studio continued to make animated shorts until 1969).[35]

In terms of short film exhibition, the formerly standardized practice of screening shorts before a feature-length film program was declining by the early 1950s, with both long-term and wide-ranging repercussions. Looking back from a 1967 vantage point, Derrick Knight and Vincent Porter recalled the impact the Paramount decree had in England: "Rumour had it that theatrical short film-making was now virtually non-existent. . . . Now [in 1967] that production is divorced from exhibition, the market for short films in the U.S.A. is minimal. Whatever the benefits of preventing vertical integration within the industry may be, this form of legislation alone is of very little benefit to the short film-maker. The feature film is the main attraction in the cinema."[36] Certainly, it is well known that the tradition of screening short films theatrically before a feature film (or two) was more and more rare starting in the 1950s, but film historians have told us more about the effects on the production and exhibition of the feature-length film. Less well known is that when the studios began closing their shorts units, short film production became a largely independent and student endeavor, and shorts found favor at film festivals and in 16 mm distribution markets. At the same time, the fiction short's range of running times expanded, and fiction shorts began to register the influence of avant-garde films (which also were usually short). Due to these and other developments, the late 1950s and 1960s proved to be an era of impressive change and renewal for the short film.

Film Schools and Shorts

In 1947, *Hollywood Quarterly* quoted a prediction made by Will Hays, head of the Motion Picture Producers and Distributors Association, regarding the influence universities would likely have in the future: "Recognition of the motion picture as an art by the great universities [will mark] the beginning of a new day in motion picture work. It [will pave] the way for the motion picture's Shakespeares."[37] Hays's prediction came true in the post-studio era, when several film schools were founded in the United States. The development proved to be one of the most significant factors in short film history, as the production of shorts became an essential component of the curriculum for student filmmakers. The institutions that inaugurated film-production related curricula include the University of California, Los Angeles's (UCLA) film school founded in 1947; Northwestern University's film program in 1956; and the film programs launched at New York University's (NYU) Tisch School of the Arts and Columbia University in 1965. Also significantly, the proliferation of film schools and programs took place on a global level.[38] Nationally and internationally, students flocked to the new film schools and programs, and shorts enjoyed a boost as thousands of student films were made, several of which found success off-campus.

Recently, in a much-needed addition to film and media studies, Duncan Petrie has addressed the historical importance of the new film programs. As he notes, after the dismantling of the studio system in the United States, film schools took the lead in training new filmmakers: "The move from a model of in-house factory production to a more diffuse system of one-off projects created the opportunity for university [programs] to assume an enhanced role as the training ground for aspiring feature film-makers."[39] Likewise, the film critic

Emanuel Levy observed that "When the studio system, previously the de facto academy for filmmakers, was disintegrating, schools began to fill the void."[40] By the late 1960s and early 1970s, several film-school–educated directors associated with the "new Hollywood cinema" era, like Martin Scorsese (NYU) and George Lucas (University of Southern California [USC]), had achieved success as feature-length filmmakers, and critics often addressed the importance of their student shorts in their development and differences from their studio predecessors. Levy, for example, argues that film schools became "a powerful force for rejuvenating Hollywood."[41] They were also a powerful force for rejuvenating the short film.

Starting in the mid-1960s, there was considerable attention in the mainstream press to film students and their contributions to film culture. At least a few writers were inspired to use the term "explosion" to register their impressions of the growth in film schools and students. In 1968, for example, *Time* magazine observed the recent increases in student filmmakers and singled out the programs at USC, UCLA, and NYU as exceptional in turning out graduates with the skills to make films of "professional quality," which they had demonstrated in their short films.[42] There were even a few observers who confessed to being overwhelmed by the sheer numbers of shorts produced by students. In 1966, *Film Quarterly*'s Jackson Burgess bemoaned the critic's inability to stay on top of student shorts, because in "the past two or three years, [the volume is] so large that nobody can keep up with it, not even the professors." Nevertheless, Burgess insisted that student shorts had value and "deserve to be taken seriously."[43] In 1973, the Academy of Motion Picture Arts and Sciences did just that, by inaugurating the Student Academy Awards in order "to support and encourage excellence in filmmaking at the collegiate level." The first awards ceremony, held in December 1973, was a high-profile event hosted by Jack Lemmon.[44]

Further testament to the serious attention student films and filmmakers received at the time is provided by a 1970 monograph, *Films on the Campus*, which is a survey of sixteen university film programs in the United States. According to the author, Thomas Fensch, his efforts were inspired by the "explosion in film interest on the nation's campuses," which he predicted would "not only continue, but increase, in the coming months and years." In his aim to provide an understanding of "the student film world as it exists today," he conducted extensive campus interviews with students and faculty, and viewed of over five hundred student films.[45] Although its attention to the individual schools is somewhat idiosyncratic, *Films on the Campus* is fascinating for its discussions of several student films that Fensch claimed were indicative of the preferred pedagogical approaches and filmmaking trends at each of the schools. Fensch was especially interested in the students and shorts that had found success by screening and winning awards at off-campus film festivals, and he commended the faculty of USC and UCLA for encouraging students to submit their work to festivals.[46] Of course, the schools also benefited as festival awards brought prestige to them as well as their students. Fensch singled out George Lucas and his legendary thesis short *Electronic Labyrinth THX 1138 4EB* (1967) for special praise and included both in his chapter title, "The University of Southern California: The Crew Concept; Lucas and *THX*." Characterizing Lucas as one of USC's "finest" graduates, Fensch provided considerable biographical information about his educational trajectory, along with a fairly detailed production history of *Labyrinth*, which he praised as "the best student science-fiction film ever made." As evidence, he cited several of Lucas's festival awards, including those from the National Student Film Festival, the Edinburgh International Film Festival, and Germany's highly regarded International Short Film Festival Oberhausen. He further noted that *Labyrinth* had been well received at several university and other nontheatrical venues, was reviewed in *Time* magazine, and had become renowned among student filmmakers inspired by Lucas's success, including the news that he was adapting it for the more simply but still enigmatically titled feature-length film *THX 1138* (1971).[47]

The widespread fascination with student shorts in the 1960s is also suggested by the many important screening opportunities held at on-campus and off-campus events. At UCLA, public showcases of student shorts were advertised and reviewed by the local press and attracted capacity crowds to the campus's 1800-seat Royce Hall. Likewise, the Ann Arbor Film Festival was a prestigious event for student film-makers because it provided the added benefit of a touring program of award-winning shorts that screened at universities, other film festivals, and theatrically at some city venues.[48] The competitive National Student Film Festival was a particularly high-profile event; inaugurated in 1965, it was cosponsored by the Motion Picture Association of America, Lincoln Center for the Performing Arts, and the US National Student Association. *Film Quarterly*'s reviewer cited the festival as evidence that "many new young artists on campuses around the country are making sharp, carefully edited films full of special effects and full of determination to avoid clichés."[49] The festival achieved a higher profile, in 1968, when its award-winning shorts enjoyed additional festival exposure, including at Oberhausen.[50] Other prestigious venues and awards for student shorts included the Producers Guild of America's Intercollegiate Awards in Los Angeles, the International Student Film Festival in Amsterdam, and NYU's annual Haig Manoogian Screening held in Los Angeles.

There was also great attention to the work of film students at international universities during the 1960s and 1970s. An interesting case study is provided by Roman Polanski's history as a film student at the Lodz Film School, which is routinely cited in discussions of his career; it's also a subject that Polanski has addressed in extensive detail. In a lengthy profile in *The New York Times*, for example, Polanski praised the rigor and intensity of his university's curriculum, saying: "The schooling is amazingly thorough . . . By the time you finish, you are making your own short films."[51] In his autobiography, he carefully delineated the film production requirements as follows: "In the course of their five years student directors were required to make at least two one-minute silent shorts, a ten- or fifteen-minute documentary, a dramatized film of the same length, and, finally, a 'diploma' film that could run for even longer. Opportunities for further filmmaking were almost limitless, however."[52] Due perhaps to his early acclaim as a student filmmaker, Polanski's shorts are among the best known in film history. He completed several, both as a student and early in his professional career—before and after his highly regarded feature-length film *Knife in the Water* (1962), including *Breaking Up the Dance* (1957), *When Angels Fall* (1959), *The Fat and the Lean* (1961), and *Mammals* (1962). Not surprisingly, the most often addressed title is his first award-winning student short *Two Men and a Wardrobe* (1958) (which is discussed below and in chapter five herein). In several different *New York Times* articles, for example, *Two Men* is cited as evidence of the director's early success and recurring interest in, as one journalist's profile put it, "the inconsequentialities, the non sequiturs, the essential absurdity, [and] the madness of existence."[53] Unlike many successful feature-length film directors, Polanski himself has often spoken about his short films, and in considerable detail. In the United States, perhaps the only director to share Polanski's regard for his short films is Martin Scorsese.

Film Festivals and Shorts

Like college and university film courses and programs, the significance of film festivals to short films after the end of the studio system cannot be overestimated. In the 1960s and 1970s, theatrical screenings of short films had become so rare that a former shorts producer, Pete Smith, jokingly lamented: "Today a short in a theater is practically as rare as a tick on a rubber duck."[54] Addressing the infrequency of theatrical screenings, *The New York Times*'s Renata Adler blamed theater owners who rented "advertising shorts" for lower fees than those charged for "legitimate shorts" and either chose to screen the commercial shorts or excluded shorts altogether. Adler considered the situation so dire that she issued a warning that theatrically screened shorts were in danger of becoming "extinct," despite what she insisted was enormous and growing public interest in them.[55] In the context of such limited opportunities, the attention shorts received at film festivals was not only welcome but also arguably crucial to the survival and viability of the form.

Starting in the 1950s, film festivals showcased and provided important alternatives to regular theatrical screenings for shorts. Several international events invited and celebrated shorts, including Cannes, which awarded its first Palme d'Or Award for short film in 1955. In addition to the inclusion of short film screenings at features-oriented events, several important shorts-only festivals were founded. The world's oldest short film festival, Germany's International Short Film Festival Oberhausen, held its first edition in 1954. Considered one of the world's preeminent shorts festivals, Oberhausen was founded with the mandate to provide an alternative to the "standardized film products appearing in commercial cinemas."[56] Toward that end, it soon earned a reputation for programming ambitious "ideologically and aesthetically diverse" shorts that elicited passionate debate and admiration from film enthusiasts and filmmakers.[57] The festival's reach and significance to aspiring and student filmmakers was confirmed in 1962 when a group of young German radicals and would-be filmmakers delivered their "Oberhausen Manifesto" during the festival and declared: "The old film is dead. We believe in the new one." They specifically acknowledged their commitment to the short form because they had been inspired by the films they'd seen at Oberhausen, which reflected the new trends and styles of non-German filmmakers associated with the European New Waves, like Alain Resnais, Francois Truffaut, Jean-Luc Godard, and Roman Polanski.[58] The International Festival of Short Films at Tours (in France), launched in 1956, was another high-profile event, that Jean-Luc Godard made a point to review in the late 1950s as part of his critic's duties for *Cahiers du Cinéma*.

One short in particular seized the attention of young cinephiles at the international festivals: *The Red Balloon/Le Ballon Rouge* (Lamorisse, 1956). Heide Fehrenbach has noted that it was enthusiastically received at Germany's Mannheim Film Festival and was identified as one of the titles that inspired awareness among young filmmakers about what was taking place in short filmmaking outside of Germany. As Fehrenbach explains, *The Red Balloon* "provoked an incredibly enthusiastic response from the Mannheim festival audience.

Such a response . . . was at once encouraging and depressing because it illustrated the audience's sophisticated understanding of the film medium but also demonstrated just how 'hopeless' the state of the German film industry was."[59] It was also festivals that launched Roman Polanski's filmmaking reputation, when his offbeat and now-legendary student short, *Two Men and a Wardrobe*, enjoyed successful screenings. After winning the bronze medal at the Brussels World Fair, *Two Men* screened at Oberhausen where it won an Honorable Mention Award and at the San Francisco International Film Festival where it won the Golden Gate Award. Further, as Polanski recalled in his autobiography, it was the first student short to be commercially released in Poland.[60]

Since the 1980s, short films have benefited from the global proliferation of film festivals, both those dedicated exclusively to shorts and the features-oriented events that include programs of shorts, like Cannes and Sundance. Today, the online festival submission site Withoutabox lists 359 online and on-site shorts-only festivals. The two most prestigious shorts-only festivals are Germany's International Short Film Festival Oberhausen and France's Clermont-Ferrand International Short Film Festival, which became a competitive event in 1982. Oberhausen focuses both on new international works (including competitive programs), in addition to shorts from throughout cinema history, which are screened in themed programs, retrospectives, profiles of individual filmmakers and film institutions (such as film schools and production companies), and guest-curated events. Clermont-Ferrand, like Oberhausen, features both old and new titles, along with special profiles, showcases, retrospectives, and panels and seminars.[61] Another high-profile festival, Australia's Tropfest claims to be the "world's largest short film festival," with live events and satellite feeds in the United States, France, India, and China (among others).[62] Recent noteworthy developments in the short film festival landscape include events that make a selection of officially programmed shorts available online too, including Sundance and the Palm Springs International Shortfest.

16 mm Nontheatrical Distribution

Also starting in the 1950s, short films enjoyed success in the expanding realm of 16 mm nontheatrical and educational film distribution. In the United States, the easier availability of 16 mm projection equipment enabled the widespread distribution of short films to primary and secondary schools, colleges and universities, and other nontheatrical venues. The situation was ideal for some student filmmakers because 16 mm was the gauge preferred by film schools, and still is, in many cases.[63] In addition, there was considerable government support for educational films. As Geoff Alexander's research demonstrates, the 1965 federal Elementary and Secondary Education Act "made millions of dollars available to schools for educational materials, which included films. Film companies created a whirlwind of new films, and hired young filmmakers . . . to make them." Unfortunately, for 16 mm film enthusiasts and distributors, the educational and nontheatrical distribution network was nearly obsolete by the mid-1980s, due to the burgeoning consumer-centered videotape industry.[64]

1970s and Beyond

Certainly, film festivals and nontheatrical film distributors provided important screening opportunities for short films, although far fewer than during the studio era. Additionally, some space was provided for short films, starting in the 1970s, with the growth of cable television outlets. For example, Home Box Office (now HBO), which was launched in limited markets in 1972, programmed shorts between feature-length films so that the features would begin on the hour, and The Movie Channel, in the 1980s, programmed live-action and animated shorts in its "Reel Shorts" program. Later, in the 1990s, Showtime offered the "30-Minute Movie" series, and today it offers shorts online in its "Short Stories" category.[65] Starting in 1981, with the launch of MTV, the shorts terrain shifted as some aspiring filmmakers made music videos instead of fiction shorts; however, the network occasionally programmed fiction shorts too, including the animated work of Bill Plympton in the 1980s. Other television broadcasters and cable outlets that have screened short films are PBS, BET, AMC, IFC, the Sundance Channel, and Logo. But even with the availability of shorts on cable and broadcast television in the 1970s and 1980s, the opportunities to see and screen shorts were very limited in the United States and remained so until the late 1990s.

Soon after the introduction of DVDs in the 1990s, a number of short film compilations were released. Among the noteworthy collections are the "Cinema 16" series, with separate discs devoted to American, British, World, and European shorts; the annual "Academy Award Nominated Shorts"; and the "Short Cinema Journal" series. Although rare, individual shorts have also been released on DVD, including *George Lucas in Love* (Nussbaum, 1999). Likewise, occasionally collections devoted to individual filmmakers with extensive shorts filmographies have been released on DVD, including those featuring the work of Spike Jonze, Chris Cunningham, and Michel Gondry. More numerous on DVD are feature-length omnibus and anthology short film collections, both old and new, including *Quartet* (1949), a collection of Somerset Maugham adaptations; *O. Henry's Full House* (1952); *Lumiere and Company* (1995); *Coffee and Cigarettes* (2003); *Eros* (2004); and *Five* (2011). Recently, DVD short film collections have been produced less frequently and, in some cases, including the annual "Academy Award Nominated Shorts," they have migrated to online sites, like iTunes.

By far, however, the single most important factor in terms of enabling the widespread availability of and attention to short films is the development of online distribution strategies. In the early period of online availability, shorts benefited, relative to feature-length films, because their smaller files made for easier downloading and streaming. But the biggest bonanza for shorts has been the development of faster, higher quality content streaming and the introduction of online platforms, both free and fee-based, such as YouTube, iTunes, and Vimeo. There were a few hiccups along the way, however. In the early days of streaming, the launch of AtomFilms, in 1999, promised greater short film availability. As *Variety* reported at the time, the company's aim was "to establish itself at the center of the burgeoning young-talent scene that's producing short films and animation."[66] In addition to licensing content for various cable outlets, like Sundance and HBO, and assorted other venues, AtomFilms' primary focus was upon offering online access to live-action, animated, and series-based shorts. AtomFilms did not fulfill its online mission, despite various marketing and international expansion efforts (primarily to Europe), mostly because it failed to find a way to profitably monetize its online content.[67] AtomFilms has become a legendary example of the setback for shorts in the early era of Internet streaming; as film programmer Roberta Munroe recalled: "There was a time not too long ago in the hyperridiculous dot-com era when every online hub and its corporate parent threw wads of cash at short filmmakers. . . . Big companies like BMW and Chrysler got in on the craze too, making their own short films. . . . We were in the bubble and the future looked bright. . . . And then we woke up. Everybody realized streaming blew . . . and the venture-capital dough vanished."[68]

But soon, of course, YouTube and other online platforms for short films changed all that. By far, the boom time in short film availability and media convergence began when the video-sharing site YouTube was launched in 2005. YouTube has enabled the short film, both old and new, not only to emerge from the margins but also, arguably, to enjoy a higher profile than ever before. In 2008, the *Los Angeles Times* noted the significance of YouTube for the increased visibility of shorts, especially among younger viewers: "Thanks to a new generation of viewers more conversant with YouTube than with appointment television, the short subject seems to be making a comeback."[69] YouTube is now the go-to source for live-action fiction shorts (among many others, of course), and many of the shorts mentioned in this volume are available on the site.

Today, shorts are the most available and perhaps popular form on the Internet. Further, in terms of the fiction short specifically, there are many sites devoted specifically to it, including online shorts festivals, curated video-sharing sites, and blogs. Another fascinating aspect of today's short film landscape is one that echoes the early silent cinema era in some uncanny ways. Specifically, with the introduction of the so-called fourth screens, such as iPods, tablets, laptops, and smart phones, as one writer has observed, "solitary viewing on the internet is not so far removed from Edison's Kinetoscope."[70]

3

Short Film Specificity: Narrative Compression, Unity, Character, and Endings

In 1959, Jean-Luc Godard issued a provocative yet ambivalent declaration about the short film and its "essence." He said it had none. Writing for *Cahiers du Cinéma* in his capacity as reviewer of the French Festival of Short Films at Tours, and in his typically acerbic and cheeky way, Godard both dismissed the short film and then recuperated it. He first insisted that critics were "wrong to believe in some special function of the short film" and, speaking for his *Cahiers* colleagues too, he confessed: "none of us has ever believed that on the one hand there was the short film with its principles and aesthetic possibilities, and on the other the feature, with other principles and other aesthetic possibilities." He quickly qualified his claims, however, with a larger conclusion: "For there is no difference in kind between a short film and a feature, only . . . in degree. Or rather, there shouldn't be. But there is." His reasoning seems to have been that the short film's brevity prevents it from dealing "in depth" with a subject because, in comparison to the feature-length film, "a short film does not have the time to *think*." In other words, he seemed to consider the form's chief limitation to be its inability to provide access to character subjectivity and depth of knowledge. He therefore concluded that the short film functions as "anti-cinema," like the "antibody in medicine,"

to strengthen the "cinema."[1] Although it's difficult to pin down precisely what Godard meant by "strengthen," he went on to praise several shorts he had seen at the Tours festival, including a few titles by
his French cohorts Agnes Varda, Jacques Demy, and Alain Resnais. It's
also worth noting that, not only had Godard made several shorts by
1959, he would go on to make several more.

Godard's efforts to get at the short film's essence by considering
its differences from the feature-length film suggest the challenges
other critics and short film writers have encountered in their own
work. Indeed, writers have been compelled to specify the differences
between shorts and features by means of various analogies that, while
not as bold as Godard's "antibody," refer to other forms, especially
literary and visual ones. Jack Ofield, for example, emphasizes the issue
of scale in his suggestion that "The short film is to the feature film
what chamber music is to the symphony, haiku to epic verse, the min-
iature to the mural."[2] Likewise, Ian Lewis observes that short films are
"not just long films that are short. . . . If a conventional feature film is
like a novel or a symphony, then a short is more like a short story—or
even a poem, [or] a song. A short story is not just a novel in 15 pages
instead of 250. The form is quite different. The aims are quite
different."[3] Most common, by far, are analogies between the short
film and the short story. Unfortunately, in most cases, analogies are
deployed as though the differences they are meant to illuminate are
self-evident, so claims about the short film like "the form is quite different" are not explained further. That is, other than suggesting broad
differences related to size, running time, or length, those that involve
issues related to storytelling in particular usually remain unaddressed.

The purpose of this chapter is to consider the elements that are
most consistently found and specific to the short fiction film, especially those related to unity, character, and endings. The examination
of the short film's specificity is substantially assisted by the work of
short story theorists, especially by their discussions of short form storytelling and the identification of unity as one of the story's most
distinctive components. In addition to the theoretical links between
the short story and short film discussed below, there is a compelling

historical connection too. As historian Kristin Thompson has noted, the short story provided an important model of unified storytelling during the early period of the transition to the feature-length film, between 1909 and 1917, as narratives became longer and more complex. Most significantly, the short story's tendency to focus on only one or two central characters and a single compelling situation or event was well deployed in many one-reel and two-reel films.[4]

Unity

In 1968, Renata Adler, a *New York Times* film critic, argued that the many strengths and pleasures of short films include that they are "likely to be superior to the features they accompany [because] shorts without the cumbersome apparatus of features . . . can be made with a particular unity and coherence out of a single mind and imagination . . . They are more likely to be of a piece."[5] Adler's reference to unity is significant, as it's one of the most frequently cited conceptualizations of short form storytelling, and it enables a careful distinction between the short and the feature. In classical Hollywood's feature-length film the concept of narrative unity refers to the careful interweaving of more than one storyline into a coherent whole to ease viewer understanding. As David Bordwell and Kristin Thompson explain, "When all the relationships we perceive within a film are clear and economically interwoven, we say that the film has *unity*. We call a unified film tight, because there seem to be no gaps in the formal relationships."[6] In the short fiction film, the concept of unity refers to something else entirely: economical and narrowly focused narratives. In general, the fiction short refuses the feature film's elaborately developed plots, subplots, goal-oriented characters, and complex causal chains. Instead, the short favors the narrative economy and unity that are enabled by its most basic storytelling conventions: a simple story that focuses on a single event, character, situation, or moment with no subplots; fewer characters—usually only one or two central characters with few (or no) secondary characters; and a brief story time.

Literary theory's attention to the relationship between brevity and unity in the short story is especially helpful for distinguishing the short from the feature-length film. Story theorists typically consider the concept of unity as a definitive aspect of short storytelling. It is unity that inspired Brander Matthews to observe, much like Ian Lewis above, that the short story "is something other and something more than a mere story which is short."[7] The American author Edgar Allan Poe is credited with introducing the concept of unity to story theory; also considered the very first short story theorist, he made the case that the short story is a distinct narrative form that is profoundly different from the novel.[8] For Poe, the essential difference between the novel and short story is the latter's "unity of effect," which is achieved by means of a rigorous narrative economy and the focus on a specific event or situation. He also favored story unity for its potential to enable narrative intensity and advised authors accordingly; arguing that unity "is a point of the greatest importance," he explained that without it "the deepest effects," "high excitements," "immense force," and "singular power" of the short form "cannot be brought about."[9] Not surprisingly, for a writer known for his own short stories, Poe considered unity a beneficial result of a well-crafted story's narrative compression, and he furthermore dismissed the novel as "verbose," "ponderous," "inaccessible," and antithetical to such unity and intensity.[10] Indeed, for Poe, there was a "direct ratio" between a work's brevity and its intensity.[11] His fellow short story author Anton Chekhov agreed, saying it is "compactness that makes short things alive."[12] Brander Matthews likewise endorsed Poe's insistence on narrative compression and unity with his own observation that "a short story deals with a single character, a single event, a single emotion, or the series of emotions called forth by a single situation."[13] Mary Louise Pratt put it even more simply: "The short story deals with a single thing, the novel with many things."[14]

Often the single thing in both the short story and the short film is a carefully selected fragment of time that evokes the spontaneity, ephemerality, beauty, or singularity of a passing moment—or a "slice of life"—unbound by the demands of causality. Short story theorists have identified the value of a well-chosen moment, including Poe who favored stories built on "a fragment upon which the whole turned"; Charles May who observed the importance of focusing "on a moment of time that meaningfully breaks up the routine of everyday reality"; and Georg Lukács who noted the preference of short story writers for the fragment that "pin-points the strangeness and ambiguity of life." Likewise, as literary theorist Wendell Harris argues, the essence of the short story depends upon the carefully delimited moment whose purpose "is to isolate, to portray the individual person, or moment, or scene in isolation—detached from the great continuum—at once social and historical . . . The short story is indeed the natural vehicle for the presentation of . . . the moment whose intensity makes it seem outside the ordinary stream of time . . . or outside our ordinary range of experience."[15] The award-winning filmmaker Lynne Ramsay has addressed her own interest in capturing smaller but memorable moments in shorts: "nothing is ever going to be the same again . . . but they're tiny moments."[16] The attention to singular moments and slice-of-life narratives is characteristic of the classical and art short, and it is an enduring aspect of the live-action fiction short, as the discussions of *Trifles* and *The Hard Guy* in chapter two (herein) suggest. In addition, the emphasis on narrative fragments in many short films has a profound effect on the kinds of characters and stories that tend to be favored, as this chapter's film analyses demonstrate.

Like the short story, the short fiction film tends to favor economical, narrowly focused narratives that work in the service of intensity, especially intense endings. As both are short storytelling forms, it is unsurprising that several short film discourses, like story theorists, place a similar emphasis on compression and unity in order to distinguish the short from the feature-length film. Perhaps most impressively, during a lecture to filmmakers in 1941, Sergei Eisenstein, filmmaker, teacher, and theorist, endorsed the short fiction film specifically as a mode of production and expression, and he used the short story to make his points. Eisenstein acknowledged his own unheeded call in the 1920s for a university group to be convened in order to "analyse the composition of the short fictional film. . . . No one has dealt with it in either theory or practice."[17] Notably, without using the term "unity" explicitly, Eisenstein nevertheless alluded to the concept in his discussion of American short story author Ambrose Bierce's attention to careful narrative focus and refusal of multiple storylines and characters. As Eisenstein explained (emphasis added), Bierce "usually *highlighted* the horror and cruelty of war. [His] method is very *simple*: on the one hand, he *compresses* the horror . . . and on the other, he debunks certain literary traditions—the extolling of military characters, heroic young women, and notorious front line camaraderie."[18] In identifying the distinguishing characteristics of the short fiction film, Eisenstein favored what he called "micro-dramaturgy" and "condensed dramaturgical solutions," which also sounds very much like story theory's unity and narrative compression.[19]

As noted above, although subsequent film writers have claimed that the fiction short has characteristics that distinguish it from the feature-length fiction film, they typically provide no further support. However, a few writers have alluded to the concept of unity and the short film's dependence upon narrative compression; for example, manual authors Pat Cooper and Ken Dancyger convey the notion of unity in their advice to screenwriters that the short film is "best" when it achieves "a level of compression of character and plot that often strengthens the uniqueness of the premise." Likewise, film teacher Symon Quy asserts that the "quintessential" quality of shorts is their "effective realization of one particular idea."[20] Journalist Gareth Evans makes a similar point but rather more poetically with his claim that the "best" short films are "crystalline creations of precise, prismatic intensity."[21] Such observations regarding the concept of unity and the corresponding differences between the feature-length and the short films have historical dimensions too. As Kristin Thompson observes, in the transition to the feature-length film it became evident that it "was not simply an expanded one-reeler," and that the two forms had different "structural principles." Those principles include narrative compression and the "single impression," which the shorter form achieved by means of the focus on a "single, central dominant incident."[22]

The short fiction film's commitment to unity is suggested by the variety of ways in which it achieves narrative compression by means of the focus on a "single thing," including a carefully delimited slice-of-life moment. Although this is not an exhaustive list of the recurring scenarios that enable the short film's unity, in general, the fiction short's most consistent scenarios, structures, and patterns, which often work in combination, include the following: the daily routine that results in an unexpected outcome (*Joe, Aadan, The Lift*, and *The Big Shave*); the ritual occasion and preparation for it (*The Man Without a Head* and *Cracker Bag*); a brief and continuous stretch of time (*Wind* and *After Rain*); a brief relationship conveyed in its entirety, as in the chance encounter between two strangers (*Two Cars, One Night, How They Get There*, and *The Lunch Date*); a single conversation (*Dinner Conversation*); a short journey (*Rendezvous* and *They Caught the Ferry*); and a small-scale quest (*Five Feet High and Rising*). The short fiction film's narrative compression by means of the focus on single events and situations not only serves its unity but also, arguably, its pleasure, which upcoming analyses will demonstrate. In addition to the longer analysis of *About a Girl* that closes this chapter, several of the strategies will be addressed in analyses of selected titles in both the classic and art short categories; however, it is useful to briefly address a few here.

A Palme d'Or winner at Cannes, the Hungarian short *After Rain/ Esö Után* (Meszaros, 2002) is a strong example of an art short whose spare narrative is built upon a combination of strategies: the short journey and a brief and continuous stretch—or fragment—of time. A shorter short, with a four-minute running time, *After Rain* focuses upon an elusive yet intense narrative moment, in which a young woman rides a bicycle along a wet, rural road, while a man calls to her from the doorway of a small house. The woman continues riding until she falls, examines a large bruise on her thigh, then gets up, and returns to the house as the film ends—so her attempted escape (if that is indeed what it was) is only temporary. Less attuned to plot than to mood, and ambiguous as to meanings, *After Rain*'s unity is a result of the focus on two characters during a precisely delimited moment. *After Rain* also supports William Phillips's claim that brevity can serve more "challenging and subtle" short films that are open to many interpretations.[23] The brief, continuous moment is so common in the fiction short that Quy characterizes it as "a snapshot of a moment in time."[24]

In terms of other strategies for conveying a compact focus on a single thing, the Canadian art short *Aadan* (Nadda, 2004) features a daily ritual, shown more than once, that produces an unexpected outcome. The protagonist is a young Muslim woman who leaves her office tower, places her prayer rug on the grass in a crowded city park, and begins to pray, which elicits the curious gazes of a few onlookers and hostile remarks from others. The second time the young woman begins to pray in the same spot, the nasty comments begin again and tension builds until another young woman responds to the hostility by joining the first woman to pray alongside her. Finally, the third time the young woman prays, several other strangers are inspired to join her and the film ends with a wide shot of a large and diverse group of people praying together in an entirely peaceful park.

Martin Scorsese's art short *The Big Shave* (1968) also features the daily routine that produces an unexpected result, in this case, a surreal one. The story is very spare, the time is continuous, and it has only one character and one action: shaving. After a series of shots of a pristine and shiny white bathroom, a young man enters and begins to shave. Soon, the routine act becomes nightmarish as he cuts himself, but apparently not accidentally, because he remains expressionless and continues shaving and cutting until he has seriously bloodied himself, the sink, and the floor.

Character and Characterization

Shorts construct characters, especially protagonists, in markedly different ways than feature-length films. For one thing, although substantial character development is conventional for protagonists in classical Hollywood's features, characters in both classical and art shorts are more loosely constructed and usually remain unchanged. There is also often an elusiveness and ambiguity about characters in

shorts due to the form's conventional emphasis on narrative economy and the de-emphasis on exposition. Perhaps most significantly,
the short film protagonist tends *not* to be driven by specific, clearly
defined goals. Indeed, the short fiction film's dependence upon simple stories typically precludes the complicated plot development that
ensues when protagonists struggle to achieve primary (and often secondary) goals and encounter obstacles along the way, especially in the
form of antagonists with their own competing goals. Not surprisingly,
such observations echo literary theorists who note a similar tendency
in the short story, including Paul March-Russell who explains that
the story protagonist "is not necessarily suited to character development."[25] Certainly, the short film's narrative compression and limited,
often continuous, story duration supports abbreviated characterization. Even the main characters in shorts have a limited number of
clearly defined traits, which are established with quick strokes. It's
an aspect of the short fiction film that Eisenstein addressed when he
advised filmmakers that characters should have no more than two
or three distinctive traits.[26] Likewise, as Richard Raskin points out,
"there is just enough time to establish the attributes of each character
and little room for the transformation of any one of them, especially
when screen-time and story-time are identical, as is often the case. . . .
[So] change in the sense of the inner growth and development of the
main character is beyond the range of the short fiction film."[27]

The spare character development in the short film relates to another
remarkable contrast with the feature film: there are few heroes (or
winners) in the short film. Indeed, on the very rare occasions when
there is tangible character success, or even triumph, it is generally not
heroic. Short story author and theorist, Frank O'Connor, has made
a striking claim with regard to heroic figures in short storytelling:
"In fact, the short story has never had a hero." For March-Russell,
a key factor is the typical brevity of story time, because characters
"cannot age and develop . . . but are suspended at a single point in
their lives," which certainly precludes the kinds of large-scale actions
that are usually required for heroic action.[28] Cooper and Dancyger
make a similar point with regard to the short film, which they also

relate to the brevity of the form: "heroic action is less credible in the short film, because of its scale."[29] In contrast to the feature film protagonists who tend to be rather more complex and undergo important change and development, protagonists in shorts usually do not change significantly, even if their experiences are dramatic. As Patrick Nash notes, the short usually lacks the "transformational arc" characteristic of feature film protagonists.[30] Certainly, without a protagonist determined to accomplish a specific goal and to do so in the face of inevitable and often overwhelming challenges and antagonists, the short film tends to enable neither extraordinary success nor heroism.

Short film protagonists tend also to be more isolated and marginalized than their feature film counterparts. The short's frequent focus on a single character, which serves the purpose of unity, is often realized in protagonists who are lonely and marginalized in some way. Although largely unaddressed by short film writers, literary theorists have examined the short story's common preference for lonely often outsider characters. Frank O'Connor is credited with being the first to call attention to and identify such characters as a defining element of short storytelling practices; in his aptly titled classic *The Lonely Voice*, he issued his most often-quoted claim: "Always in the short story there is this sense of outlawed figures wandering about the fringes of society . . . As a result there is in the short story at its most characteristic something we do not often find in the novel—an intense awareness of human loneliness."[31] To make the point, he proposes a key character type, the "little man," which he illustrates by referencing the tormented, long-suffering protagonist of the Nikolai Gogol short story "The Overcoat" from 1842. Very briefly, the story concerns protagonist Akakey Akakeivitch, an impoverished copy-clerk whose overcoat is so worn and threadbare it provides no protection from the cold. Even worse, his young colleagues mock him relentlessly about it. When his tailor insists the old coat is beyond repair, the clerk finally agrees to order a new one and is overjoyed when he receives it. But his happiness is short lived, as the overcoat is quickly stolen and soon thereafter the clerk dies as he has lived—alone. For O'Connor, although one may sympathize with such an isolated, lonely protagonist, one is not encouraged to identify with him as with a more active, decisive, and successful character.[32]

Spare character development produces another narrative effect in the short film: love stories are perhaps as scarce as heroes. Although the love story is a persistent narrative element of the feature-length film, love and romance rarely play a prominent—or any—part in the short's narrative. The key factor, of course, is the short's most characteristic feature—its brevity. As David Bordwell notes, classical Hollywood's feature-length films usually have two storylines, one of which involves heterosexual romance.[33] Further, Kristin Thompson has identified a link between running time and the attention to love or romance in her research on the transition to the multiple-reel, feature-length film between 1909 and 1917; as she explains, as films became longer, "the greater length . . . gave the romance more prominence."[34] Likewise, in the short story there are fewer love and romance tales too. Noting that a story's potential subject matter is related to length, story theorist Brander Matthews addressed the contrast between the short story and novel, concluding that the short form is stronger because it does not depend upon love-based narrative threads to provide a kind of connective tissue:

> While the Novel cannot get on easily without love, the Short story can. Since love seems to be almost the only thing which will give interest to a long story, the writer of Novels has to get love into his tales as best he may . . . But the short story, being brief, does not need a love-interest to hold its parts together, and the writer of Short stories has thus a greater freedom.[35]

In the case of the short fiction film, even when love and romance are a focus of the narrative, it usually doesn't lead to the familiar feature-length film ending in which the couple lives "happily ever after."

In the live-action fiction short, unlike the feature-length film, protagonists are rarely active narrative agents driven to achieve specific goals, but are more often reactive. Thus, a common short film scenario concerns a protagonist at a pivotal moment—usually unexpected— whose situation demands a decision or choice. Story theorist Pratt characterizes the "moment of truth" strategy as one that presents "a single point of crisis in the life of a central character, a crisis which provokes some basic realization that will change the character's life forever."[36] Certainly, feature film protagonists often experience unexpected circumstances and must make choices about them; the difference in the fiction short is that the pivotal moment and response constitute the core of the plot. Cooper and Dancyger endorse the strategy's effectiveness in simple narratives; echoing Pratt, they argue that the short "works best when its plot is uncomplicated, when we are given a glimpse of someone at a particular—very likely pivotal— moment in his or her life, a moment when an incident or a simple choice sets in motion a chain of events."[37] Not surprisingly, the pivotal moments range from those that call for minor choices to more life-threatening ones.

The Palme d'Or nominated short *Joe* (Wolf, 1997) is a sly comedy that falls at the less dramatic end of the choice spectrum. *Joe's* titular protagonist is a patient in a mental institution who seems to spend much of his time polishing his beautiful black boots and then proudly wearing them in the common room. The unexpected occurs when a jittery fellow patient inadvertently and unknowingly spills his Maalox on one of Joe's boots. Tension builds as Joe, whose particular malady is unknown and could involve aggression or something equally unpleasant or dangerous, sees the damage. Tension continues to build when Joe returns to his room and, because he is shot from behind, his response is unclear—until his task is complete. His choice, which underscores the film's comedic intentions as well as the significance of this pivotal moment, is to adapt by making his boots even better—by entirely coating them with the Maalox and transforming them into beautiful white boots. A far more dramatic and horrifying pivotal moment occurs in the longer and more complex film, with a moral crisis at its center, *Most* (Garabedian, 2003). The protagonist is a young single father who works as a drawbridge tender. When he takes his eight-year-old son to work and tells him to stay well away from the bridge until the next train passes, the father proceeds to wait for the coming train. When he fails to notice the imminent arrival of the too early train, and also fails to see his son trying to warn him about it, the boy falls into the bridge's gears, and the desperate father must make a quick decision—to either save his son's life or the lives of the train's many passengers.[38]

Endings

The differences between short and feature films include their approaches to endings: in the short fiction film they tend to be more intense. It's a strategy they share with short stories, so literary theorists' observations about them as a characteristic tendency are instructive. They generally agree that, compared to novels, story endings carry more weight. As May observes, in short fiction, "it is the end that lends significance to all that preceded it."[39] Edgar Allan Poe considered endings so vital to the short story's unity that he advised authors to begin writing only after they had a precise ending in mind. As he explained, "If [the] very initial sentence [does not bring out] this preconceived effect, then [the writer] has failed."[40] Manual writers have likewise noted that short film endings carry more narrative weight or intensity than is the case in feature films. Echoing Poe's notions regarding endings, Nash advises aspiring writers that "The best way to open your screenplay is to know your ending so you can work towards it, planting the right cues, orchestrating . . . conflict and so on."[41] Similarly, Clifford Thurlow advises filmmakers more simply to "find the ending; then the beginning."[42] As for the short form's preference for highly intense endings, May explains, "there is no way to deny that the shortness of the form seems inevitably to require some sense of intensity or intensification of structure and emphasis on the end— a requirement that is absent in the novel."[43] B. M. Éjxenbaum similarly emphasizes the power of the short story's ending with a striking set of analogies; as he argues, the story "amasses its whole weight *toward the ending*. Like a bomb dropped from an airplane." Although surprise endings are rare in novels, because they typically involve "a point of let-up and not of intensification," Éjxenbaum notes the short story's tendency to gravitate "expressly toward maximal unexpectedness of a finale concentrating around itself all that has preceded. . . . [It's like] a climb up a mountain the aim of which is a view from on high."[44] Like short stories, the short film's preference for intense endings is often the result of surprises. They are so common that Eisenstein addressed their significance and favorably contrasted them with what he deemed the "typical, talentless treatment of a subject," in which "[e]verything is clear . . . And there are no shocks to be had."[45]

In short film analyses, one may distinguish between two different kinds of unexpected endings: the "surprise" and the "twist." Although each depends upon the presentation of something unexpected, the surprise ending involves something that has not happened yet, so neither the viewer nor any of the characters can anticipate it with certainty. The term "surprise" is useful because the unexpected event is a surprise to everyone—characters and viewers alike. In contrast, the twist ending involves the climactic revelation of some key piece of story knowledge that has been withheld from the viewer and therefore produces a shift—or twist—in expectations about possible outcomes. In other words, the twist ending depends upon the viewer's limited range of knowledge about crucial story information that could have been made available earlier. Manual author Nash conveys the effect by referring to the twist ending as a "revelation ending."[46]

The distinction between the surprise and twist ending in the short fiction film can be demonstrated with a few examples. A compelling use of the surprise ending occurs in the nine-minute Australian short *Spider* (Edgerton, 2007), which actually features two surprises. *Spider*'s protagonist is a well-meaning but not particularly sensitive young man who tries to ingratiate himself during a road trip with his angry girlfriend by secretly buying her flowers and chocolate—and a plastic spider. When he hides the spider in the car's sun visor, one certainly expects it will produce a bad result, but there is a surprise nonetheless. When the girlfriend pulls down the visor and the plastic spider pops out, she panics, stops the car, and leaps out, whereupon the boyfriend makes another unfortunate move when he tosses the spider to her to show her it's a fake and, startled yet again, she jumps backward into the street and—surprise—she is immediately slammed by an oncoming car. This surprise sets up the next: as paramedics tend to the injured girlfriend, one of them lifts her arm for an injection, and the spider is exposed again. The paramedic then gets spooked, jumps backward, and accidentally stabs the boyfriend in the eye with the hypodermic needle, which looks rather comically like a dart stuck in a board. Although both of *Spider*'s surprises involve events that are unexpected by viewers and characters, the second surprise results in an even more intense ending, in part, because it plays for laughs by recalling the film's prescient prologue: "It's all fun and games until someone loses an eye."

Before moving to examples of the twist ending, it is useful to relate it to Bordwell's concept of the "suppressed gap," which refers to the unexpected and delayed revelation to the viewer of story knowledge that could have been made available earlier. Only when the suppressed gap is revealed does the viewer become aware that the omitted information is necessary to fully understand the story, which encourages a reconsideration of the narrative's development in light of it. When the elided material is especially significant, despite that it has ranked low on the viewer's scale of probabilities, it can serve to finally reveal the crux of the story.[47] Eisenstein refers to the twist ending as a preferred method for delivering intense endings that "shock." Insisting that effective endings must be both "unexpected and sharp," he favors the withholding of significant story information until a short film's end so that the viewer will not have "even the slightest hint of any other explanation."[48]

Of course, the twist ending also is occasionally used in feature films, such as *Fight Club* (Fincher, 1999) and *The Crying Game* (Jordan, 1992), but it is far more common in the fiction short and tends to be considered a short film convention. The strategy is used in a darkly comic way in the four-minute *Desserts* (Stark, 1999), in which a young man walking along a deserted beach happens upon a delicious-looking éclair sitting atop the sand. After looking around for a moment, presumably to see if the sweet belongs to anyone, he proceeds to take a bite that reveals the giant fishhook hidden inside by some unknown entity, which becomes lodged in his cheek. The film ends as he is dragged violently out to sea, thus revealing the story's mainspring and the reason for the title's plural form—this is a tale of apparently sweet revenge for some giant unseen sea creature.

One of the most famous short film twist endings occurs in the adaptation of the Ambrose Bierce short story, *An Occurrence at Owl Creek Bridge* (Enrico, 1962). Set during the Civil War, it begins with a young man on a gallows being readied for execution as punishment for tampering with a bridge. After the trapdoor is pulled and he drops into the river below, the man apparently survives and manages to escape by swimming and then running away in the direction of his home. He has almost reached the arms of his waiting wife when the twist is revealed: his execution has been successful after all, and his escape and journey have been products of his imagination. The intensity of this twist ending is due to the several minutes of screen time during which we share moments of the man's subjectivity and are thus unaware of both the reality of his situation, which has transpired in mere seconds, and that we have been misled about the passage of time. It is worth noting that, as these surprise and twist examples suggest, such endings are often also violent, which certainly adds to their intensity. But, whether violent or not, the twist strategy is so common in the short fiction film that some filmmakers have addressed both its frequency and usefulness as a storytelling strategy. Among those in favor of the device is filmmaker Danielle Lurie who observes: "Most filmmakers are under the impression that for a short film to work, it needs to have an excellent twist at the end—and I agree with that."[49] On the other hand, filmmaker Lynne Ramsay has acknowledged that because the twist ending has become so predictable, she avoids it in her own short films.[50]

Certainly, not all short fiction films include intense endings. Furthermore, they are not limited to those of the surprise or twist variety, although they may still offer something unexpected. At the end of the classic short *The Red Balloon* (Lamorisse, 1956), for example, after a little boy's balloon companion is destroyed, he is lifted high into the sky by dozens of balloons that have flown to his side in order to console and to lift him, literally, from his gloom.

Film Analysis: *About a Girl*

The usefulness of the concepts of unity, intensity, and narrative compression for clarifying the specificity of the short fiction film and its distinctive treatment of character and endings are well demonstrated with an analysis of the ten-minute film, *About a Girl* (Percival, 2001). A British title, *Girl* is a dynamic, thoughtful, and beautifully acted art short that screened at several festivals and won the British Academy of Film and Television Arts Award for "Best Short Film." It is also a challenging film, both for its provocative content and bold style. A character-driven rather than plot-driven film, its fragmented structure includes several flashbacks and jump cuts, and alternates sequences of direct character address with more conventional ones that observe the "fourth wall" between the characters and audience. Its unity is the result of a tight focus on its unnamed protagonist, the thirteen-year-old "Girl."

The majority of the film shows the Girl as she walks alone through her working-class town and along a canal while speaking in direct address and with some bravado to the camera/viewer about her dreams for the future and her troubled relationship with her family. The monologue sequences have a fast pace due to several stylistic details: the Girl's rapid delivery, a pattern of jump cuts, and the brief flashbacks presented as fragments that show her with her friends on the bus goofing off and singing the Britney Spears's "Oops! . . . I Did It Again" song, in her neighborhood with her single mother and siblings, and with her unemployed, disinterested father at his soccer game and afterwards at a pub. Along with her monologue, the flashbacks seem to provide considerable exposition about the Girl who appears to be fairly conventional in terms of her preoccupation with popular culture and celebrities, her desire to be "dear rich and famous" like her idol Britney Spears, and to be seen as older, especially by her father. Most importantly, the Girl seems not to be motivated by an immediate and specific goal until the film's intense, unexpected, and shattering ending. After describing the time her mother recruited the neighbors to drown the Girl's new puppy in the canal, she confesses that "I've gotten dead good at hiding things from her since then," whereupon she tosses a plastic shopping bag into the canal and an underwater shot reveals the dead newborn baby that has been hidden inside. Thus, we finally learn that hers has been a short-term, goal-oriented journey after all, which provokes the further realization that we actually know very little about this girl, including her name. Many questions remain unanswered, which adds further to the intensity of the ending, such as Whose baby?, How was it conceived?, How was it delivered?, and so forth. In addition, even before the revelation of the ending, despite the Girl's sounding both confident and irreverent during her monologue, the circumstances of her life belie her posturing and plans for the future.

Girl also conveys the loneliness of its protagonist that is common to the short fiction film. Most significant are the three longer-duration shots that contrast with the quicker rhythms of the direct address sequences and that show her alone as she sings lyrics from the Britney Spears's song "Stronger." *Girl* is bookended by two such shots. The film's very first shot shows her on a grassy hill singing and dancing confidently (see Figure 3.1). It's a dramatic image as she's framed from a low angle in silhouette against a cloudy sky, which might suggest a bold—perhaps heroic—spirit. The film's last image, however, poses a

Figure 3.1 *About a Girl* (2001)

stark contrast to the first: a high- and wide-angle crane shot, it shows her walking along the deserted canal away from the camera as she sings very quietly, underscoring her youth and heartbreakingly lonely secret. Finally, the shot that occurs between these two shows the Girl alone as she sits on a public bench waiting for her father. As she moves her feet and sings quietly, the camera zooms from a medium- to a wide-shot to reveal that she's sitting entirely alone in the middle of a small patch of grass. The loneliness of the moment is emphasized by the offscreen sounds of a boisterous and likely drunk bunch of men, including her father, singing together in the nearby pub. During each of the three shots, the Girl sings the same lyrics from the "Stronger" song, which specifically reference loneliness: "But now I'm stronger than yesterday. Now it's nothing but my way. My loneliness ain't killing me no more." By the film's end, the lyrics from this anthem of self-empowerment finally seem tragically ironic for the Girl.

About a Girl demonstrates that the profound fascination and pleasure of the short fiction film is enabled by its unity and careful narrative compression; in just under ten minutes, the film presents a richly detailed and compelling—yet elusive—portrait of a character that neither changes nor triumphs during the course of a brief and lonely journey that leads to an intense twist ending. The next two chapters consider several titles in the classical and art short categories that provide further evidence of the power and pleasures of the short fiction film.

4

Storytelling and Style:
The Classical Short

Since David Bordwell, Janet Staiger, and Kristin Thompson introduced the immensely useful, painstakingly researched volume,
The Classical Hollywood Cinema, their paradigm of the classical narrative mode has enabled the systematic study of feature-length films.
It also has served as a useful point of comparison for films that do not
fit the classical mode, such as the live-action fiction short. Briefly, the
classical Hollywood film narrative turns on a causal chain motivated
by a protagonist's desire to achieve a particular goal, whose efforts
are countered by an antagonist, which produces conflict and leads to
a closed ending in which the fate of the characters, their goals, and
the outcome of their conflicts are clear.[1] The majority of short fiction
films do not to adhere to the classical Hollywood narrative model
with its elaborately developed characters, plots, and subplots. In
addition, unlike feature-length films, shorts rarely portray heroes or
extraordinary triumphs; there are fewer love stories; and endings tend
to be more intense, as noted in chapter three (herein). This chapter
organizes the classical short according to several variations including,
in the most general terms, storytelling strategies that range from simple to more complex, and from short to long, with running times that
range from a few minutes up to an hour. Not surprisingly, running
time tends to correlate with narrative complexity, especially in the
classical short. Thus, the "shorter short," of five minutes or less, favors

rudimentary stories that unfold in real time, often in a single location, and they very often use narrative strategies that were prominent during the early silent cinema era, especially the gag and the "attraction." In contrast, the longer short, with a running time between twenty and sixty minutes, tends to be more highly plotted with the occasional subplot, but without the elaborate integration of multiple storylines, characters, and character development of classical Hollywood's feature-length film.

The classical short shares the live-action fiction short's typical preferences for simple stories without subplots that focus on a single event or situation during a brief story time. In general, classical shorts have easily discerned meanings and transparent situations, linear organizations, and closed endings. In addition, characters tend to have clear goals and motivations, and to be drawn broadly, usually because they are based on familiar types or stereotypes, which enables compact characterization. It's a set of strategies manual writers tend to endorse. Ric Beairsto, for example, is adamant that although life can be "messy, scary at times, full of loose ends and unresolved problems . . . we demand that a story be tidy, that all conflicts be resolved in the end."[2] Likewise, story theorist Mary Rohrberger's conception of the "simple short narrative" is useful for understanding the classical short, regardless of length: "There are no mysteries to be solved, no depths to be plumbed. Meaning is apparent, [and] easily articulated."[3] Certainly, such a description may also apply to the feature-length film, but the short film's unity is a key differentiating factor. Further, the easy meanings of the classical short are well represented in the genre short, which uses a limited number of the narrative and visual conventions of its feature-length film counterparts. Although the art short category includes genre titles, they are somewhat more common in the classical category.

The following discussion includes attention to individual shorts from throughout film history, though there is some emphasis on shorts from the studio era when classical shorts were the dominant category. In addition, the discussion is intended to demonstrate an historical difference between classical shorts from Hollywood's studio era and post-studio titles; the former tend to be set bound and formally conservative, whereas the latter deploy a wider range of storytelling and formal strategies. It also demonstrates that the classical short's focused and easy-to-grasp narratives and characters have enabled a compelling range of content and styles, including those that suggest the legacy of several silent era strategies. Finally, the discussion is intended to counter the impulse in film criticism and scholarship to overlook classical shorts in favor of art shorts—although festival programmers and manual authors appreciate a broader range of stories and styles, including those with mainstream or wider appeal.

Prenarrative "Attractions"

The discussion of the classical short begins with the most rudimentary and spare narrative possibilities, which reflect an important legacy of the short's early silent forebears. Indeed, several recent short films feature visual and storytelling elements that convey the continuing appeal of strategies used in the earliest motion pictures. Certainly more compelling than the routine observation that, in the beginning, all films were short is that some of the early silent cinema's strategies have endured in the short form. Before a consideration of the specific narrative conventions of the classical short film, it is helpful to address a few of the nonnarrative strategies that were common in early motion pictures. Film historian Tom Gunning's conception of what he calls the "cinema of attraction" is especially useful. Dominant until about 1907, two key components of attraction-based films are the "ability to *show* something" and the "exhibitionist impulse to acknowledge the audience" when performers look directly into the camera. In other words, as Gunning notes, "early cinema was not dominated by the narrative impulse" but rather by the aim to present "a series of views to an audience." Also significantly, the cinema of attraction mode did not disappear but rather went "underground"—to the avant garde and some narrative films, including fiction shorts. As the following examples suggest, like the early attraction films, several contemporary titles convey the compelling possibilities of a "freedom from the creation of a diegesis."[4]

The award-winning short *The Dance Lesson/La Leçon de Danse* (Prouff, 2006) is a fascinating recent example of the continuing inclination to show something while acknowledging the audience. It also recalls the "comic views" category identified by Gunning, in which an amusing scene is presented without narrative motivation.[5] *Lesson* is five minutes long and consists entirely of one long-duration, fixed-frame wide shot. After a young man walks into a small dark room that looks a bit like a den, he positions himself in the center of the frame, pauses to remove his T-shirt, and walks closer to the camera so he's framed from the thighs up. While looking into and facing the camera, he stretches a bit and audibly cracks a few of his joints. He then spends two minutes demonstrating a series of gestures and poses as the sometimes funny names of the moves are superimposed at the bottom of the screen, including "big fish," "small fish," "stirring the soup," "rollercoaster," "leading the revolution," and so on. At about the mid-point of the film, the man steps back into the shot's background, so that his full body is again visible, whereupon a disco ball is lowered into the space and he turns on a boom box that plays percussive, upbeat dance music. As the disco ball and holiday-style lights begin flashing, he puts all his offbeat poses and gestures together, in the order in which he demonstrated them, to perform a very dynamic and amusing dance. Although it has comedic intentions and is more elaborate with its two-part lesson-and-dance structure, *The Dance Lesson* recalls the Edison studio's well-known attraction-style dance films, including the best-known *Serpentine Dance* from the mid-1890s, which shows a young woman in a single, nearly one-minute-long straight-on shot seductively using her arms to make the voluminous fabric of her long dress undulate.

Claude Lelouch's 1976 short *Rendezvous/C'était un Rendezvous* likewise demonstrates the attraction impulse to "show something"; more precisely, it recalls early silent era films that showcase landscapes and scenery from the perspective of a moving vehicle.[6] *Rendezvous* develops a variation, however, as it has a very rudimentary narrative (as the title promises). Accompanied by the shrill, ambient sounds of screeching tires and a revving engine, *Rendezvous* shows the city of Paris at dawn in a single nearly nine-minute-long shot made from the perspective of an unseen (until the very end) driver as he careens wildly from one end of Paris to the other, ignoring red lights and traffic lines, so there are some chilling near-misses with other vehicles and pedestrians along the way.[7] Not until the last few seconds of the film, when the driver screeches to a stop and jumps out to kiss a young woman, is it revealed that his goal during the exhilarating and sometimes hair-raising drive has been to make it to their "rendezvous" (see Figure 4.1). Certainly, *Rendezvous* fulfills the cinema of attraction aim to provide "exciting spectacles" that produce "shock or surprise," rather than "narrative absorption."[8] In addition to being one of the better-known shorts in film history, *Rendezvous* has inspired several fans to recreate it in their own single-shot driving films, some of which are posted online.

Figure 4.1   *Rendezvous* (1976)

Rudimentary Narratives: The Gag

At the simplest end of the narrative spectrum, the gag is among the most enduring short film strategies and is especially suited to films with shorter running times—because gags are economical and deliver their laughs or jolts quickly using limited character and plot development. As film historian Gunning quipped, by way of some Shakespearian inspiration: "Brevity is the soul of the gag."[9] The continuing appeal of the gag structure for short filmmakers is what made it ideal for early silent filmmakers—its narrative and visual simplicity. The gag-centered short depends upon the most rudimentary narratives, which one scholar has characterized as "micronarratives."[10] The Lumiere brothers' *The Waterer Watered/L'Arroseur Arrosé* (1895) remains the original—both the earliest and best-known gag film, it is inspired in its narrative compression, unity, and visual design. In what is likely the most often described plot in film history, *Waterer* deploys a single gag, in a single wide shot, in which a man in the midst of watering his garden with a hose is interrupted when a rascal steps on the hose and stops the flow, until the gardener investigates by looking into the nozzle whereupon the rascal releases the flow and the gardener's face gets doused, though the rascal gets his comeuppance when the gardener gives chase. As film historians often note, not only is *Waterer* the earliest fictional narrative, it's also the first film comedy. Gunning identifies *Waterer* as the gag film prototype that inspired a full-fledged genre with far-reaching effects. As he explains, the earliest gag films consist of a single shot, have short running times, and depict a "bit of mischief" that involves a rascal and an intended victim, and which use a precise yet basic two-step narrative pattern with a "mischievous preparation and laughable consequence."[11]

Three recent shorts convey the continuing appeal of the gag structure; the first two examples are dialogue free, like their early cinema precursors. Although they are not one-shot films, their narratives unfold in continuous time. The four-minute short *Desserts* (Stark, 1998) (also discussed in chapter three, herein, in relation to the twist ending) uses a bit of surreality in its demonstration of the virtues of the simple gag narrative without dialogue. It also fits Gunning's "connection devices" category, in which the gag depends upon a rascal who somehow schemes to link a victim to an object "with a bit of string."[12] In this case, *Desserts'* victim is hooked to a fishing line when he bites into an apparently unattended éclair and he's dragged out to sea by an unseen rascal. Another dialogue-free gag film, the three-minute *The Black Hole* (Sansom and Williams, 2008), also deploys a bit of surreality as the rascal in this case is a copy machine that produces a sheet of paper with a solid black hole that enables the tired office drone who discovers it to reach through solid surfaces. After using the hole to steal a candy bar from a vending machine, the soon-to-be victim quickly decides to use the magic black hole to steal a pile of cash from a locked safe. But the fun ends for the thief when he crawls through the door to gather more money and his hastily taped black hole falls off, which traps him inside, while the copier registers its satisfaction with some offscreen chirping. In a more good-natured, dialogue-based gag short, the three-minute *Sign Language* (Sharp, 2010) uses a documentary style to tell the story of a colorful and enthusiastic young sign holder in London who addresses the camera to introduce his fellow sign holders and to explain that it's his last day on the job. At the end of his shift, the protagonist looks wistful as he confesses that he thought his co-workers might give him "a send off or something." The bit of mischief is revealed when the other sign holders turn their signs around one by one to reveal that they have conspired to deliver a sweet good-bye message and a bit of helpful romantic advice.

The gag structure is also well represented in recent longer comedies too, as it was during the silent era. As Kristine Karnick and Henry Jenkins have observed, as comedies became longer in the 1910s, they were often episodic with an "accordion-like structure," in which a situation could be easily expanded with an extended gag sequence. *Signing Off* (Sarkies, 1997) uses the strategy in the service of a fast-paced, fifteen-minute narrative that moves breathlessly from one climax to the next. In this case, the gag does not involve a rascal's prank but rather the action-and-reaction structure identified by

Karnick and Jenkins.[13] The series of gags in *Signing Off* is only loosely dependent upon plot and is initiated when the protagonist, an elderly disc jockey just fired for being out of touch with modern listeners, accidentally drops the last record he intends to play on his last-ever show for a faithful and nostalgic elderly listener. Along with a rapid pace and a deadline structure assisted by silent era style crosscutting between the disc jockey and his fan, the protagonist's maladroit move initiates a cascading chain of complications that involves a relentless series of obstacles, including a giant street sweeper—when the record lands in the gutter, a rat-filled city drainpipe, and a stairwell filled with a swarm of employees trying to escape the explosion and fire he's unintentionally started—all of which the disc jockey overcomes with deft physical feats. Finally, in a bit of luck, the record lands on the platter just in time for the show's last song, whereupon the twist is revealed: his listener has fallen asleep.

Simple Shorts

As one moves along the scale of storytelling complexity in the live-action fiction short, from simpler to more complex, the trajectory in many ways echoes formal and storytelling developments from the early silent era to the mid-1910s, when the feature-length film became the dominant studio form. This narrative trajectory is perhaps even more fascinating for its enduring representation in the short film. The key narrative developments involve the transition from single scenes made with, at first, a single shot and then multiple shots, to narratives with multiple shots and multiple scenes; and, in terms of causality, as narratives moved from an early design that was situation rather than character based and the focus was on telling a clear and logical story "in which an initial cause [often an accident] produced a chain of effects which ended in a 'satisfactory' resolution," to a more complex design in which a causal chain is activated by developed, individualized characters acting on their desires to achieve specific goals.[14] Edward Branigan's conceptualization of the episode is useful for characterizing the simple short; describing the episode as a narrative that collects "everything that happens to a particular character in a particular setting as well as everything that the character does in that setting," he notes that an episode also shows change and development as it progresses.[15] As the following analyses demonstrate, the short's narrative continuum, from simple to complex, has enabled a long history of storytelling. In addition to observing the frequency of genre-based shorts, the discussion also is intended to reflect several narrative structures and strategies that are particularly common in the live-action fiction short, including the journey, the single meeting or conversation, the brief relationship, and the attention to a specific social issue.

Omnibus (Karmann, 1992) is a simple eight-minute-long French comedy that features a journey, and whose easy appeal is suggested by the fact that it won the Academy Award, Palme d'Or at Cannes, and the British Academy of Film and Television Arts Award. After boarding a commuter train for his journey to a brand new job, the protagonist soon learns, to his horror, that the train has a new schedule and will no longer stop at his desired destination. The commuter desperately tries to convince the conductor and driver to let him disembark at his usual station; but, instead of stopping, the driver slows down enough for the man to jump. Then, in a sequence worthy of a silent comedy, the man manages to land successfully, but when he runs alongside the train to keep his momentum going—so he won't fall over—another commuter misunderstands his intention and "helps" him by lifting him back onto the train. Another simple short, the comedy *Inside-Out* (Guard and Guard, 1999) features what looks like the beginning of a romance, which plays out entirely without dialogue and with a combination of humor and pathos that recalls Charlie Chaplin's silent comedies. Its simple narrative concerns a brief relationship, from beginning to end, between two young people—he's a survey worker and she's a window dresser—in the midst of busy London who have an amusing exchange despite being separated by a plate glass window. As the young man strikes out again and again in his efforts to recruit passersby for his survey, the young woman works on her window display and watches him with some amusement. When he catches her eye, he flirts by performing a few silent-style comedy antics, which apparently win her over. But theirs is a temporary romance that is thwarted when they move just enough so they can no longer see each other through the window, and the film concludes with each walking off-screen in opposite directions. Finally, in the simple short *Dinner Conversation* (Cashman, 2005)—one of the few fiction shorts with a bona fide love story—the low-budget, skit-style romantic comedy depicts a brief, continuous-time conversation between two young men, one of whom is hosting the other for dinner. With great economy, their conversation provides just enough exposition to establish that they are in the early stages of a dating relationship. After a string of compliments about the meal, the guest unintentionally blurts out "I love you," and the snappy dialogue that ensues achieves screwball comedy proportions until the host confesses, also unintentionally, "I love you too," whereupon the duo decides to seal the deal by moving in together.

Moving further along the complexity continuum, Carl Theodor Dreyer's *They Caught the Ferry/De Naade Faergen* (1948) is easy to understand in its focus on a short-term journey that is slightly more complex due to the suspense generated by its deadline structure and the inclusion of a few horror film moments. Made as a Danish road safety film, it features a young couple on a motorcycle who want to catch a ferry in a dangerously limited time. Along with the looming deadline, the film's tension is enabled by a condensed narrative in which more than forty-five minutes of story time is conveyed in twelve minutes of screen time. Using dialogue very sparingly, *Ferry* begins in medias res as the couple waits to disembark from a ferry so they can quickly drive across an island to catch another ferry, despite a worker's warning that the road they'll take has many curves and the journey will be seventy-five kilometers, which is all but impossible in the forty-five minutes they have. Before they're off the first ferry, a dose of doom is added to the mix because the couple's motorcycle is positioned ominously close to a spooky, big, black hearse, which they will encounter—as an antagonist—a few times during their journey. The couple's ride is both harrowing and thrilling as they speed through the countryside on the winding road, while weaving recklessly back and forth to pass motorized vehicles, horse-drawn carriages, and livestock. Much of the trip is conveyed from the couple's point of view, including several insert shots of the motorcycle's speedometer, which underscores their wildly excessive speed. Tension builds further when they stop to get gas and, most dramatically, when they later pass the hearse and a closer shot reveals that the driver looks rather ghoulish in expression and pallor. Next, they make the wrong choice at a fork in the road and spend precious time turning around, so the hearse gets ahead of them again. As they near the end of their journey, the couple tries to pass the hearse once more but they slam into a tree, which is made more dramatic with slow-motion imagery (see Figure 4.2). In the end, the title proves ironic, as the last shots reveal that the couple has "caught the ferry"—by way of their coffins. Although there are some subtleties in *Ferry*'s visual design, including the use of point-of-view shots that enhance the narrative suspense, its meanings are both simple and forthright.

Figure 4.2   *They Caught the Ferry* (1948)

The next example concerns another historically noteworthy short *The House I Live In* (LeRoy, 1944), whose narrative involves a single, conversation-based meeting, and demonstrates the easy-to-grasp narrative strategies and the set-bound style common to Hollywood's studio era shorts. *House* is noteworthy for several other reasons too: it's a social issue film produced during the Second World War that addresses anti-Semitism, and it was directed by Mervyn LeRoy and stars Frank Sinatra. Described as a "tolerance short subject," the production studio, RKO, announced that it was "designed to advance Americanism through better social understanding," and all profits would be contributed to "organizations working to combat juvenile delinquency."[16] It also won a special Academy Award that was presented to Sinatra in 1945, and in 2007 it was added to the Library of Congress's National Film Registry. *House* has a very simple, eleven-minute continuous-time narrative that uses one location to present an easily grasped homily about religious (though not racist) hatred delivered by musical star and up-and-coming movie star Sinatra, playing himself. It opens with Sinatra and a full orchestra at the beginning of a recording session for a song performed in its entirety. Then, as he steps into the alley for a cigarette, Sinatra happens upon a gang of boys tormenting another boy who's Jewish; as the singer intervenes to protect the boy one of the bullies declares, "We don't like his religion." At that point, Sinatra gets the bullies' angry attention by first calling them "Nazis" and then softens them with a lesson that turns into an anecdote about the successful bombing of a "Jap" battleship, which includes the detail that one of the team was Jewish. Sinatra's conclusion: if the heroic bombers had been "stupid" enough to fight each other because of their different religions, they would have failed in their shared mission to fight the enemy and thereby protect "this wonderful country." Sinatra seals the deal by singing a patriotic song, also in its entirety. His own mission accomplished, Sinatra says goodbye to the "men" as they—and their new Jewish friend—go on their way. With a narrative that focuses precisely on the presentation of a problem and its quick resolution, *House* apparently made its point. Indeed, it was recalled nostalgically by a film distributor who had been persuaded, much like the gang of bullies in the film: "Viewing [it] helped shape my own intolerance towards racism and hatred. It was that powerful. And it was not a feature film. It was a short."[17]

Although relatively short, at four minutes, Eva Saks's *Confection* (2003) features a fanciful meeting between two disparate strangers, which is simple yet slightly more complex in its evocation of its protagonist's subjectivity. Made to honor New York City in the wake of the 9/11 tragedy, *Confection* features a sweet and earnest but not sentimental tale told from the perspective of a little girl on an excursion in the city with her mother, while accompanied diegetically and nondiegetically by Tchaikovsky's "Dance of the Sugar Plum Fairy."[18] After making a difficult bakery decision about which beautiful pastry she wants, the girl carries her strawberry-laden confection carefully while walking with her cell-phone distracted mother and being amused by a few adult passersby on the street. When a homeless man reaches out to her, the girl pulls the sweet closer to her body and keeps moving. But when she spots a poster for the City Ballet she stops in her tracks, whereupon her fantasy of being a beloved ballerina is shown briefly. The sound of her mother's voice brings her back to reality where she finds herself in mid-pose and, as her mother leads her away, the off-screen sound of someone clapping catches her attention; when she turns she discovers it's the homeless man applauding her impromptu "performance." Smiling, the girl dashes back to the man and gallantly presents him with her pastry, and the two exchange irresistible smiles before her mother pulls her away.

Longer Shorts

Classical shorts with longer running times sometimes more closely follow the narrative mode of classical Hollywood's feature film. As Andrew Lund notes, "longer shorts boast some real benefits. They provide the opportunity for character development, narrative arc, three-act structure, subplots, . . . genre conventions, and many other cinematic and narrative tools commonly employed by the feature filmmaker."[19] The work of short story theorist March-Russell is useful for understanding and appreciating the benefits of classical shorts with longer running times and greater narrative complexity. Using the term "well-made story," March-Russell's project is to enable the appreciation of a mode of short storytelling that tends to be overlooked or dismissed by theorists and critics, and to counter the overwhelming preference for the more elusive, modernist stories that usually are associated with highbrow tastes. As he notes, the critical opposition to the well-made story "reveals underlying concerns, especially in the United States, surrounding the short story's cultural position, anxieties to do with taste, discernment and respectability." Specifically, the "middlebrow" well-made story develops more highly plotted narratives that are both carefully constructed and "accessibly told." March-Russell observes that such stories can be "light without being banal, crafted without being difficult, accessible without being ineloquent." As a result, although they tend to have easy-to-follow narratives, they remain open to and offer possibilities for varied interpretations. In terms of the more complex, highly designed "well-made" short film, its pleasures likewise include attention to careful patterns—repetitions, motifs, and symmetry—as well as to thematic clarity and narrative unity. In addition, protagonists tend to be more precisely developed, and while they usually do not undergo profound changes, they are nevertheless revealed in greater detail. Although they are longer and feature more complex formal strategies and stories, the well-made short remains focused on precise and economical development and thus resists the feature-length film's tendency to meander by way of secondary characters and storylines. The following discussions and analyses of longer, more complexly designed shorts not only demonstrate the characteristics of the well-made short, but also that it is a broad category that comprises a variety of styles and content.[20]

The Academy Award winner *Six Shooter* (McDonagh, 2004) is a highly plotted, twenty-seven-minute British-Irish short with high production values that combines darker story elements, including sequences of bloodshed, with comedic ones, a combination underscored by the dynamic integration of quick-fire dialogue and action-oriented sequences.[21] Its narrative complexity is due to a cast of several characters and locations, a fully developed beginning, middle, and end, and a subplot. Shot through with references to and sequences of death and bloodshed, *Six Shooter* also features a relatively rare formal strategy in shorts—the flashback, and a fairly common narrative element—a train journey. *The New York Times*'s Caryn James praised its "playfully dark humor," and called the film, "eloquent and comic, shaped by a sophisticated cinematic imagination."[22]

Donnelly, *Six Shooter*'s middle-aged protagonist, is a lonely character that mostly responds to rather than initiates events, and only loosely functions as a narrative agent. Further, although he endures and witnesses several large-scale tragic events, he does not undergo change during the course of the film. Introduced in the hospital as a doctor delivers the sad news that his wife has just died, Donnelly soon hears more tragic news about the cot deaths of two babies, and a mother whose son shot "the poor head off her." Before he makes the long journey home, Donnelly leaves a snapshot of a white rabbit with his dead wife, which suggests that he's in for a series of adventures during his journey through a dark wonderland. On the train, Donnelly sits across from a chatty and shockingly rude but also oddly entertaining young man, "Kid," who curses relentlessly while issuing a litany of insults, complaints, observations, and a vivid anecdote. Most importantly, Kid provides the subplot that drives the chain of events whereby nearly every character the largely passive Donnelly encounters has a tragic outcome, even the cow at the center of the flashback. Also significantly, the film's offbeat combination of tones includes that each of the traumatic tales and events is punctuated by moments of bitterly dry humor, much of which is the result of Kid's quick, caustic dialogue. For example, when he mentions his mother's murder the night before, he explains that he's not upset because, "Well, she wasn't the most pleasant of women, and sure, life goes on."

Six Shooter's string of tragedies begins when Kid verbally abuses the parents of one of the hospital's cot-death babies, whereupon the tormented mother commits suicide by jumping from the train. When the train gets going again, after a delay for the police investigation, Kid makes another bad move when he taunts an officer who

recognizes him as the matricidal murderer and alerts his fellow officers to be waiting at the next stop. The short journey gives Kid just
enough time to tell a *Grand Guignol* tale from the "best day" of his
childhood, which he's been itching to share, about an unfortunate
cow on display at a cattle fair who perished after her intestinal gas
was relieved and then ignited with explosively bloody results. The cow
anecdote is enacted in a flashback narrated by Kid, and its significance for him is underscored by its brightly lighted, saturated colors,
which contrast with the naturalistic color palette and mostly diffused,
lower-key lighting of the film's other sequences. The contrast is further exaggerated by the stylized rendering of the exploding cow as
pieces of what looks like cook-ready meat and streamers of red rain
down spectacularly in slow motion and are followed, finally, by the
cow's head, much to the laughing delight of the flashback Kid. When
the train reaches its next stop, the armed team of waiting police and
the Kid engage in a climactic shootout, which has Kid posing like a
Western gunfighter with a gun in each hand, and uses the quick editing and high-volume sound effects of an action movie, along with
the slow-motion cinematography and blood-filled squibs associated
with the ultraviolent aesthetic. Not surprisingly, it ends badly for the
young murderer who dies as Donnelly comforts him and while cursing his own "woeful" shooting skills. Then, seizing an opportunity,
Donnelly pockets one of Kid's guns. At home, he unexpectedly undertakes his own suicidal plan, but it backfires when he decides to use
the second-to-last bullet to shoot his wife's pet rabbit, so it won't be
orphaned, before using the last bullet on himself (see Figure 4.3). But
Donnelly has his own "tragic" ending when the gun misfires, leaving
him alive and bewildered—and even more alone at the end than at
the film's beginning. The ending is darkly comic, as Donnelly looks
directly into the camera after cursing the dumb bad luck of his day.
Further, the rabbit's return at the film's end provides a clever symmetry as it recalls the snapshot Donnelly left with his wife near the film's
beginning. That symmetry is underscored, with a bit of black humor,
because the rabbit dies like Kid's mother, without his poor head.

Figure 4.3   *Six Shooter* (2004)

The pleasures of the well-made short are demonstrated by *Six Shooter*'s complex, highly focused nonlinear plot and polished design, including its combination of comedy and drama. Like many fiction shorts, it offers troubled depictions of love, both romantic and familial. That is, although the protagonist Donnelly seems to have loved his wife very much, both his and the cot-death parents' love stories are in the past, and the Kid is not only cavalier about his dead mother he declares that if he were a parent he'd be the abusing kind, especially if "it was getting on my nerves or something." There is also some depth in the characterization of Kid, and both he and Donnelly are depicted as lonely characters. However, while Donnelly is a bit rabbity in his mostly passive reactions to Kid's rude behavior (and the rabbit might also be a leitmotif for Donnelly's character), Kid is fierce in his almost total refusal to be moved by family ties, either his own or the grieving couple's. Further, the end is doubly intense as it reveals both a twist, Donnelly's unrevealed plan to commit suicide, and a surprise when the gun misfires. The film has a careful—if cheeky—symmetry as Donnelly loses two loved ones, his wife and the rabbit, at the film's beginning and end. Although the allusion to

Alice in Wonderland's white rabbit is perhaps more subtle, the narrative is designed for easy understanding. In addition, *Six Shooter*'s unity is the result of its focus, both dramatic and comedic, on death and its many variations. Though he forgets the cow's unnatural demise, the film critic Noël Carroll tallies the film's death toll as follows: "There is a matricide, a suicide, an attempted suicide, a lethal gun battle between the police and a raving psychopath, and the assassination of a rabbit, as well as the natural deaths of one child and one wife."[23] Also, like the cow flashback's exaggerated visual style, the shootout sequence is equally stylized as Kid's bullet wounds are shown in slow motion, which enables an appreciation of their deliberately phony construction. The shared excess in both scenes also suggests Kid is in the midst of another, for him, perfect day. Furthermore, the shootout conveys yet another layer of detail and patterning, which is suggested by film critic Marshall Botvinick's observation that, "When the Kid fires on the police . . . , the scene looks like a parody of a shootout between cops and a cowboy; and when the Kid is finally gunned down in slow motion, his body, like a fountain, spouts blood in such a way that the viewer is more taken by the beauty of the shot than the horror of the death."[24]

Binta & the Great Idea/Binta y la Gran Idea (Fesser, 2004) is a well-made short with a thirty-minute running time that is rare for its well-developed subplot, cast of many characters (mostly played by nonprofessionals), and several locations. Both a visual and narrative delight, it features extraordinary cinematography and a bit of whimsical visual fancy, in which palm trees suggest fireworks—with the help of quick camera movements and zooms, and the sounds of explosions. The protagonist, Binta, is a happy Senegalese girl, about ten years old, who relates the story of her family and her village in voiceover narration. With a theme that concerns the importance of living and working together harmoniously despite differences, *Binta* also offers a moral lesson about the importance of educating girls and contrasts the smart and happy student Binta with her miserable cousin, Soda, who longs to go to school but whose father forbids it. The plot moves between Binta's storyline—which focuses primarily on her efforts to grow up to be "a wise woman" and the rehearsal and performance of the play that parallels Soda's unfortunate situation, with Binta's father's storyline—which concerns his long journey to meet with government officials in order to present his great idea about the benefits that foreign children would experience if they could spend time in Senegal. *Binta*'s two storylines also are punctuated by episodic sequences that provide texture and detail, including an upbeat montage of Binta making colorful pictures with her classmates and a flashback in which Binta's father learns more from his friend about Western notions of progress.

Binta's father is a fisherman, who is amused by his friend's tales of the "tubabs" (foreigners) who not only catch more fish and more easily with their fancy nets, boats, and equipment, but also have watches with alarms so they always know exactly what time it is. But, though he might be entertained, Binta's father is unconvinced that the tubab ways are better or that, as his friend suggests, "we should learn from them." Her father's plan is neither disclosed by him nor by Binta, in voiceover, so its revelation provides a surprise near the end of the film. Only after his complicated journey over great distances for several meetings with different government officials, and a meeting with the governor himself, does Binta's father finally present his full plan: to adopt a tubab child so that it can "acquire the knowledge necessary to be happy . . . [and] will be able to contribute to the development of humanity." *Binta*'s storyline also deals with a few more serious issues, including an episodic sequence in which Binta's aunt (and Soda's mother) is easily cheated by a conman selling her fruit because she is unable to do sums mentally. In addition, the play performed within the film underscores the necessity of educating girls by shaming those, like Soda's father, who resist the notion. Certainly, the length, complexity, and integration of the two storylines of *Binta* enables the multi-faceted yet determinedly unified development of its larger theme regarding the desirability of a future characterized by respect for people's differences and equal opportunities at both the local and global levels. For additional examples of longer, well-made shorts, see the Appendix for *The Mozart of Pickpockets/ Le Mozart des Pickpockets* (Pollet-Villard, 2006), *The Accountant* (McKinnon, 2001), and *The Tonto Woman* (Barber, 2007).

Genre Shorts

Genre shorts are common in both simpler and more complex shorts. Regardless of length, their primary difference from feature-length genre films is that, in the service of narrative economy and compression, shorts deploy fewer of the key narrative conventions of their respective genres, though they typically follow their visual conventions very closely. The most commonly represented genres in the live-action fiction short are horror, thriller, gangster, and science fiction. The following discussion demonstrates the careful design of examples from each of those genres, and each analysis suggests the strength of well-chosen yet limited genre conventions, and also conveys the symmetry, unity, and efficient construction of the well-made short.

Joyride (Gillespie, 1995) represents the slasher variety of the horror film by means of its axe-wielding killers, dark and mostly isolated locations, entrapped protagonist, and a score that echoes John Carpenter's composition for his slasher film prototype *Halloween* (1978). It has considerable intensity due in part to its clever yet spare use of slasher conventions and its brief running time. In only ten minutes, *Joyride*'s tightly focused narrative manages to be suspenseful, terrifying, and adrenaline-fueled. But, unlike the feature-length slasher film, it has no sex-obsessed teenage victims, its serial killers dispatch only two victims, both adults, and there is no "final girl" protagonist who not only survives the bloody mayhem but also kills the killer. *Joyride* begins in medias res, on a dark and stormy night, as the protagonist, an electrical line repairman, initiates a grim causal chain by shirking his professional duties and driving away from a broken, arcing power line. Almost immediately, the repairman gets kidnapped by a couple of killers who dupe him when one of them pretends to be injured in the middle of the road, whereupon they lock him in his own car trunk and take off. What follows is a chilling series of events and escalating tension as the killers proceed to murder two suspicious cops who have stopped the car (which is conveyed via offscreen sounds), and as the repairman desperately tries to untie himself in the claustrophobic trunk, which causes an open gasoline can to douse his clothing just as the trunk's electrical wiring begins to spark. The killers then crash the car in the woods while being chased by the police, and there's a brief face off between the officers and the surviving killer who tries to use the repairman as a hostage. But the repairman escapes and manages to make his way back to the police, where he has a brief chuckle when he realizes he's back where he started—at the very same broken and sparking power line he ignored at the beginning of the film. This time, however, he's wearing gasoline-soaked clothing, which ensures an explosive outcome. Although *Joyride* cheats the slasher film's conventional ending because the protagonist dies, it serves the intense surprise ending and darkly comic symmetry as the film is bookended by the same dramatic location. So, although the repairman manages to survive the killers' murderous intentions and the car crash, the causal chain he initiates by failing to do his job finally ends with his death, which is also darkly amusing because we easily anticipate the lethal results when one of the powerline's many sparks lands on him. Other noteworthy horror shorts (some of which also qualify as art shots) include *The Lift* (Zemeckis, 1972), *Kitchen Sink* (Maclean, 1989), and the zombie variations *Cargo* (Howling and Ramke, 2013) and *I Love Sarah Jane* (Susser, 2007).

In the thriller category, in addition to the journey-oriented title *They Caught the Ferry* (discussed above), *Return to Glennascaul* (Edwards, 1953) is a well-known, twenty-three-minute haunted-house short with a droll touch, in which Orson Welles, playing himself, takes a break from rehearsing his new film *Othello* to recount a "tall tale" experience he had one night while driving to Dublin. During the journey, conveyed in flashback, Welles gives a lift to a stranded man who recounts his own tall tale. The flashback within a flashback depicts the dark and rainy night when the man stopped for two stranded women and drove them to a dark and spooky house made even more ominous with canted angles, low-key lighting, and sinister compositions. But when the man returns for his forgotten lighter, he finds the house in a dilapidated state and overgrown with weeds. Upon making inquiries, he learns the incredible truth about the women—they died years before. The man's tale so unnerves

Welles that, after dropping him off, Welles swerves away from two stranded women hoping for a ride in the very same location at which he found the man with the tall tale. But things end humorously when the women recognize the actor-director but refuse to believe it's him because he would never be so "disobliging."

The science-fiction short category includes the well-known silent era French title *The Crazy Ray/Paris Qui Dort* (Clair, 1923), which is rife with location shooting in the city of Paris. A surreal fantasy, *The Crazy Ray* is also noteworthy as the French director Rene Clair's first film. A longer short, at thirty-five minutes, its fantastic story is embellished with several characters, locations, and episodes. The protagonist is a night watchman at the Eiffel Tower who awakens one morning, at precisely 3:25, to discover the city has stopped in its tracks, whereupon he makes the long descent to the bottom of the Tower to embark on a sojourn to investigate his new reality. In a lengthy sequence, the watchman is shown covering a great deal of city territory, which is conveyed in several shots that jump quickly from location to location, thus underscoring the man's initial disorientation. Though at first he encounters oddly empty streets, bridges, and parks, the watchman continues walking until he comes upon several people frozen in mid-action. The first people he finds have been frozen during routine activities, like sitting in a car or on a street bench; but as he continues, he discovers more unusual scenarios, including a man who seems to have been in the midst of committing suicide by jumping into the Seine, and a robber being chased by a cop, which inspires the man to relieve the robber of his stolen watch. The man then amuses himself by pretending to interact with a few of the frozen Parisians before taking a nap on the street, whereupon *Crazy Ray* shifts location to the airport, where a gang of just-landed tourists discover the frozen city too. Soon the tourists and watchman run into each other, and together the new friends take advantage of their irresistible opportunity by partying at an upscale nightclub, in a pond, on the various levels of the Eiffel Tower—and also by stealing items from a few perfectly unsuspecting victims. Though their antics are more mischievous than malevolent, the group's fun ends when they discover that a mad scientist, Professor Ixe, with an affinity for futurist decor and long-winded lectures is behind the "crazy ray." The ending provides a new beginning for the night watchman, and an unusual ending for a short film, as he's found a girlfriend among the tourists and she's game to see the view from his spot on the Eiffel Tower. In addition to its provocative and playful story, *Crazy Ray*'s imagery evokes the urban beauty of the "city symphony" films and includes bold high-angle shots from several Eiffel Tower vantage points, along with several street-level shots from many iconic locations throughout the city, which are amazing because the streets are overwhelmingly empty.

The gangster short includes *The Mozart of Pickpockets/Le Mozart des Pickpockets* (Pollet-Villard, 2006), which won the Academy Award as well as the Audience and Grand Prix Awards at the Clermont-Ferrand International Short Film Festival. *Mozart* is a very broad comedy with a quick pace and lively physical humor that was shot mostly on location with a mobile camera, and features the "rise and fall" convention of the gangster genre. Its protagonists are two middle-aged and artless thieves with a tired routine that involves posing as police officers in order to distract their unsuspecting victims while they lift their wallets. The pair hit a patch of bad luck when their ruse is detected, but soon they're back in the game when a deaf Romanian boy follows them and they reluctantly agree to take him into their tiny apartment. Though they fail in their attempt to include him in their criminal schemes, because the boy informs a victim about the wallet they've just stolen, the thieves discover much to their surprise and delight that the boy has the talents of a master thief. His less risky scheme involves rifling the bags of cinema patrons who are distracted by the movie onscreen instead of the little pickpocket crawling around the floor and making off with their possessions. Not surprisingly, the pair of bumbling adult thieves soon become too confident—and arrogant—about their rise in fortune, so they experience the fall that's conventional in gangster films when they pose as cops at the bowling alley because they want to quiet some loud patrons who turn out to be real cops.

Shorts and Parodies

The most common genre short, by far, is the parody. Despite the complaints of industry insiders, like programmer Sharon Badal, that "spoofs are so last century," the parody short remains popular. Moreover, it is one of the live-action fiction short's most familiar and enduring categories and has been so since the earliest days of the motion pictures.[25] To cite just one example from the early silent era, Edwin S. Porter, the Edison studio's lead filmmaker, lampooned his own hit film *The Great Train Robbery* (1903) with *The Little Train Robbery* in 1905. During the 1910s, Keystone's slapstick parodies were popular, including Mack Sennett's *Barney Oldfield's Race for a Life* (1913), which mocks the last-minute rescue of a damsel in distress that D. W. Griffith had made familiar in titles like *A Girl and Her Trust* (1912). In the 1920s, Ben Turpin starred in slapstick parodies of contemporary dramas and adventure films, including *The Shriek of Araby* (Jones, 1923).[26] As for the early sound era, such self-reflexivity remained popular, and it was associated with the fiction short in particular. Film historian Donald Crafton makes the excellent observation that the parody enabled a clear distinction between the short and the feature in a full theatrical program and did so "by adopting a satirical tone toward the main part of the program."[27] At the extreme end of the parody continuum in the early sound era is MGM's 1930s "Dogville" comedy series in which costumed dogs arranged in poses and tableaux lampoon popular movies, with the help of an explanatory voiceover. Not surprisingly, studio era short parodies were gentle and certainly promotional, if not subtle, as their titles suggest: *So Quiet on the Canine Front* (Myers, 1931) and *The Dogway Melody* (Myers, 1930).[28]

Of course, the feature-length film parody is also quite familiar and popular; nevertheless, not only is the parody more common in the short film, it's also a more diverse category. The primary difference between the two is that the feature parody is a relatively limited category because the focus is usually on a particular film genre whose conventions and permutations are exhaustively referenced, as demonstrated by the entries in the comedy franchises *Naked Gun*, which parodies the police procedural; *Airplane*, the air disaster; and *Austin Powers*, the British spy films. Shorts add to the mix by means of the wider variety of sources they reference, both individually and in combination—from literary and artistic, to commercial, industrial, and educational. As in the feature-length variety, the short parody delights in pushing its references to absurdly comedic extremes and in rewarding viewers who recognize the conventions and iconic moments that are included as well as those that are elided.[29] Further, parodies are especially suited to the short fiction film because generic and other sources can be referenced quickly and economically, which enhances their narrative unity and intensity. The short parody offers several variations, including those that focus on individual filmmakers, such as *The Dove/De Duva* (Coe and Lover, 1968), which sends up Ingmar Bergman's moody style and intimate stories. Short parodies have also focused on individual feature-length films as well as oddly comic combinations of titles and sources, as in *George Lucas in Love* (Nussbaum, 1999) and *Franz Kafka's It's a Wonderful Life* (Capaldi, 1994). In *George Lucas in Love*, *Star Wars* and its director are linked with the period romantic-comedy *Shakespeare in Love* as the USC film student Lucas struggles with a bad bout of writer's block while trying to write a science-fiction script for class. In *Franz Kafka's It's a Wonderful Life*, the dark, moody novelist suffers deeply in his efforts to begin his future classic, *The Metamorphosis*, at the same time the cheerful family downstairs is enjoying a warm—and distractingly loud—Christmas celebration.

The Oscar nominee *The Dove* is an auteur parody that mocks several of Ingmar Bergman's films and his stylistic and storytelling preoccupations, including stark black-and-white cinematography and odd framings, measured pacing, morose characters, tortured emotions, and dark and sometimes surreal situations. The dialogue is delivered in a mock Swedish dialect and is mostly English words accented with Swedish-sounding bits and English "translations," such as the first spoken words "Duva cacan" subtitled as "Dove doody." And when lesbian Sigfrid offers her cousin Inga a cigar saying, "Phallican symbol?"

the subtitle reads, "Cigar?" The Bergman films and storylines mocked in *The Dove* include its references to the protagonist's journey back home and memories of his youth from *Wild Strawberries* (1957), the game with the figure of Death in *The Seventh Seal* (1957), and the inappropriate sexual desires of *Smiles of a Summer Night* (1955). But in *The Dove*, the journey back home takes protagonist Viktor to an outhouse, the game with Death is badminton not chess, and the inappropriate lust is Viktor's for his sister Inga. The seriousness typically associated with Bergman's work is teased further with themes and motifs related to bestiality, incest, and "doody"—both bird and human.

The Bloody Olive (Bal, 1996) is a cleverly detailed and astonishingly efficient genre parody that sends up a few of the key narrative and thematic conventions of film noir, including confusing, highly complicated and ever-twisting plots that turn on duplicity, betrayal, and murder, in which viewer and character knowledge are never assured. *Olive*'s plot quickly establishes its narrative intention to present a string of murders and to cheat viewer expectations about victims, killers, and loyalty. A period film set during the original heyday of film noir in the 1940s, *Olive* also deploys the characteristic black-and-white cinematography, low-key lighting, and chiaroscuro of film noir in a tale of ever-shifting alliances and betrayals between an apparently happy husband and wife and their visiting friend, as they spend an evening beset by several apparent murders whose victims shift crazily and repeatedly. The opening montage and song use the stylized art direction and exaggerated performance styles of classical Hollywood, and are underscored by the odd song lyrics "Let's go to the movies and see a lovely show." *Olive* introduces two of the three protagonists, husband Werner and wife Mylene as they make happy, playful preparations for the Christmas holiday and celebrate their accomplishments with the beginning of a kiss that is interrupted (which recalls the interrupted kiss in Orson Welles's 1958 noir classic, *A Touch of Evil*) when the doorbell rings and Sam is invited inside. When Sam accuses Werner of embezzling company funds and demands his resignation, Werner shoots and seems to murder Sam but Sam quickly reveals that he is very much alive, which initiates the film's pattern of bogus deaths. With dizzying economy, several additional murders are committed and then quickly reversed as a series of charades are revealed. In ten minutes, nine "murders" are committed and each character is "murdered" three times, until husband and wife declare their master plan to fool Sam into a confession for an earlier murder, which is capped by another twist when concealed lawmen reveal themselves and arrest Sam. *Olive* ends with another self-conscious moment when the police superintendent—who looks and talks like a hard-boiled detective—addresses viewers directly to deliver the platitude that "crime doesn't pay" and to wish them "Merry Christmas," after which Werner and Mylene finish their interrupted kiss. Unlike feature-length films noirs, *The Bloody Olive* is organized chronologically so there are no flashbacks and, in the end, the plot has not been doom-laden, at least not for Werner and Mylene, and romantic love triumphs, which if not altogether foreign to feature-length films noirs is nonetheless rare. Of course, the pleasure of *The Bloody Olive*, as with other genre shorts, is partly due to the easy recognition of the conventions being lampooned and the dexterity of its plot twists and, for those who recognize the elided conventions, there are additional rewards.

Slasher Flick (Basile, 1999) is a silly and amusing genre parody whose appeal is partly the result of its low-budget production values, which it shares with the earliest feature-length slasher films, like *The Texas Chain Saw Massacre* (Hooper, 1974) and *Halloween* (Carpenter, 1978). Using a score that echoes Carpenter's *Halloween*, *Slasher Flick* manages to touch upon several of the key conventions in its brief twelve-minute running time, including a *Psycho*-style butcher knife, an isolated location, the use of stairwells and an elevator as suspenseful, dangerous locations, and a monster that will not die. The protagonist is a young slacker security guard at an office building who's passing the time watching a slasher movie marathon. But the film opens with a twist, as it shows black-and-white footage of a young woman in a forest being chased by a lumbering knife-wielding slasher-style monster, which is followed by the quick revelation that she and her stalker are part of the movie the protagonist is watching on an old television. *Flick* has fun mocking the popularity of its source genre when the slightly bored young marathon hostess lists so many upcoming marathon titles, including *Bride of Slasher*, *Saturday Night Slasher*, *How the Slasher Stole Christmas*, and *La Dolce Slasher*, that she puts the protagonist to sleep. *Flick* also spoofs the lurking presence of the generic slasher monster with ominous, shadowy, heavy-breathing figures that turn out to be benign. In the end, instead of a final girl, the final boy encounters a variation of the monster that refuses to die when he's chased by his own lumbering stalker in the stairwell, whom he seems to have killed with a knock-out blow, only to find yet another stalker lurking nearby. *Flick* ends as it begins with another twist that reveals the protagonist has been part of the film within a film being watched by a couple of guys in their living room, one of whom issues a quick critique, "this sucks," before changing the channel.

Herd (Mitchell, 1997) is a hilarious and rather more acerbic parody than those discussed above. A science-fiction parody with deliberately schlocky production values, *Herd* has vicious fun mocking Steven Spielberg's cute-alien in *E.T.* (1982). Its comedic intentions are conveyed immediately as the opening sequence shows plastic cow figurines being slowly lifted up to the sky in bright shafts of light. The protagonist is a burger-stand worker, Nelson, who's surprised at home one night by a little alien guy (played by a hand puppet) who enlists his help in building a complicated and mysterious black box. After the box is complete, Nelson treats his new buddy to a sightseeing excursion in Los Angeles. But the fun ends in an action-style sequence when a few tough guys haul Nelson away for a mace-enhanced interrogation about the alien, after which he's shoved into a room filled with people holding black boxes exactly like his. Meanwhile the little alien takes off in his spaceship with an "E.T. ME" license plate, which happens to be the "Googie"-style burger sculpture atop Nelson's fast-food joint. The film's twist ending reveals the alien's evil though also benevolent intentions when the black boxes assemble into a playful looking kinetic contraption that's really a bomb that destroys life on Earth. There's a happy ending though, of sorts, as the little cows are shown returning to the decimated but now burger-free landscape.

In addition to genre parodies, shorts that send up the narrative and stylistic clichés associated with particular film genres also are common. *Plot Device* (Worley, 2011), for example, mocks the conventional climaxes of several genres, each of which is depicted with its characteristic visual style and sound design as its aspiring filmmaker protagonist uses a device that drops him into a succession of films at their most sincere or worrying moments, including romantic comedy, action, noir, zombie, indie-slacker, and science-fiction films. *The Gunfighter* (Kissack, 2014) uses the Western genre's saloon setting and characters to lampoon the nondiegetic voiceover by making it diegetic, which utterly confuses and creates antagonism between the characters as they try to talk back to the unseen voice that delights in stirring up trouble.

Like feature-length parodies, shorts have lampooned a wide range of film genres; but, unlike features, they also often parody commercials, industrial films, educational films, and music videos. *Forklift Driver Klaus* (Wagner and Prehn, 2000) pushes the conventions of the industrial safety film to devastatingly comic levels of absurdity in its tale of a newly trained young forklift driver, the aptly named Klaus Berserk, who blithely ignores every safety rule endorsed by the voiceover narration, thus leaving an over-the-top trail of bloody co-workers and body parts in his wake. *The Japanese Tradition: Sushi* (Kojima, 2002) playfully mocks the conventions of educational "how-to" films, especially their penchant for detailed charts and graphs, while also gently mocking the stereotypes associated with sushi culture, and the more general Japanese preoccupation with "proper etiquette."

The Appendix includes several entries for genre shorts, in both the classical and art shorts categories. For additional genre parodies, see the entries for *7:35 in the Morning* (Vigalondo, 2003), *Epilogue* (Allen, 2013), *Je T'Aime John Wayne* (MacDonald, 2001), *So You Want to Be a Detective* (Bare, 1948), *The Heart of the World* (Maddin, 2000), and *Frankenweenie* (Burton, 1984).

5

Storytelling and Style: The Art Short

Perhaps the most profound virtue of the art short is its enormous diversity. Since its emergence in the 1950s, the art short has demonstrated a greater range of storytelling and aesthetic strategies than the classical short and, arguably, the feature-length art film. The focus in this chapter is upon the short film's conspicuous divergence during the 1950s from the more conventional plot-driven narratives, studio-bound settings, and conservative formal strategies associated with the studio era's classical short, in favor of more character-oriented, looser, episodic, and ambiguous narratives that use an array of visual strategies, from naturalistic to surreal. The early development of the art short took place in the context of the period when the film-makers associated with the influential European "New Waves" used techniques meant to counter classical Hollywood's narrative mode. As this chapter aims to demonstrate, shorts were the advance guard in the revolution. Following a brief consideration of a noteworthy precursor to the modern art short from 1933, *Zero for Conduct/Zéro de Conduit* (Vigo), the discussion will include attention to several landmark titles from the 1950s and thereafter, which help to illustrate the form's wide-ranging storytelling and formal strategies, and also convey the historical, critical, and aesthetic significance of individual films. Not surprisingly, the art short can be distinguished from the feature-length art film based on its characteristic attention to carefully focused, though often highly ambiguous, narratives and to unity.

Unlike the classical short whose narratives are generally committed to more precise cause-and-effect plotting, understandable characters, and closed endings, the art short favors ambiguity, ellipses, and tends to resist closure, definitive meanings, and superficial interpretations. In addition, the art short is often impressionist in its emphasis on tone and mood and on characters that are rarely active narrative agents and more often aimless or elusive in their motivations. Besides being more suggestive than explicit in terms of potential meanings, the art short also commonly depicts bold, thematically challenging, or otherwise unorthodox content.

The emergence and development of the art short in the 1950s is indicated by two landmark titles: *The Red Balloon/Le Ballon Rouge* (Lamorisse, 1956) and, two years later, *Two Men and a Wardrobe/ Dwaj Ludzie z Szafa* (Polanski, 1958). Both titles circulated widely at international film festivals and were early participants in and helped to pave the way for the European New Waves and international art cinema that followed. Both titles also demonstrate the formal and narrative innovations of art shorts, including their often-ambiguous and allegorical meanings. Moreover, they feature elements of fantasy and surrealism that suggest the influence of avant-garde films (which also tend to have short running times) that proved important in the subsequent development of the art short.

Before moving to an examination of the art short's emergence in the 1950s, in the context of the European New Waves, it is useful to address a significant precursor—the much earlier and now-legendary title, *Zero for Conduct*. *Zero* not only is considered a masterpiece of French cinema and beyond—Alan Williams calls it "one of the genuine masterpieces of world cinema," it also shares a number of important storytelling and stylistic preferences with its New Wave successors. *Zero* was Jean Vigo's first fiction film, which he also wrote and edited, and was based on his own grim boarding school experiences and the fierce and abiding animosity between the staff and schoolboys. It is also a longer short, at forty-four minutes, which the French refer to as a "moyen métrage" (a medium-length film of about forty-five to sixty minutes). Soon after its premiere, it was banned by the French government, presumably for its revolutionary spirit, and was not shown again until 1945. *Zero*'s loose plot consists of several amusing and sometimes odd scenes that focus on the hostilities between the school's authorities, depicted mostly as freakish caricatures, and their young charges who are given, as boys often are, both to mischief and somewhat more serious acts of rebellion. Against the relentlessly barking schoolmasters delivering or threatening "zero for conduct!," the schoolboys' only ally is the new teacher Huguet who is unruffled by the energy of the students, and is not opposed to and perhaps endorses their rebellion, much to the consternation of his superiors. The boys' antics include a food fight in response to yet another meal of beans, a slow-motion pillow fight in the dormitory, a gag-style prank that involves the "crucifixion" of a sleeping school functionary when a few boys tie the hapless victim to his bed and lift it vertically while he remains asleep, and another more aggressive rebellion at the end when the boys wreak havoc on the adults who have gathered for a public day of celebration by throwing boots, cans, and books onto them from the rooftop. It ends, however, on an ambiguous note, as the final shot shows several of the rioting boys standing atop the roof, in an odd low framing from behind the group, so it's unclear what is below or in front of them.

Zero, in its favoring of the boys' experiences and point of view, is rather like a clarion call for the free-spiritedness of youth, and also is remarkable for its refusal to focus on a singular protagonist and instead to feature a group of largely undifferentiated boys. In addition to its attention to children and youth (in Huguet), *Zero* includes strategies that would later be preferred by many European New Wave filmmakers; for example, it has an episodic organization, uses dialogue sparingly, and the boys in the cast were nonprofessional performers. Further, like *The Red Balloon* and other New Wave era shorts, *Zero* alternates between moments of naturalism and more experimental surrealist ones, as when a ball magically disappears and reappears, a line drawing becomes animated, and, during the pillow fight, when the boys' running about appears in reverse slow-motion. There is also a delightfully self-reflexive moment that references the much-beloved and often-subversive Charlie Chaplin—when the good-natured Huguet mimics the comedy star during recess to entertain the boys. Though *Zero* most often is cited for its anarchist or revolutionary sensibilities, it is significant in the context of later shorts because its meanings remain open to interpretation, including the ending that shows the boys on the roof, triumphant but as though suspended in time.[1]

The enormous significance of the French New Wave on feature filmmaking is, of course, well documented in scholarly and critical discourses; however, the ways in which short films figured in the revolution—and influenced or enabled it, and continued to be inspired by it, remain mostly unaddressed. As is well known in film history, during the mid-1950s, many new and often young European filmmakers were committed to making films that challenged the status quo. The shorts they made both reflected that commitment and further inspired them to experiment with storytelling and formal strategies. For the French New Wave specifically, critics-turned-directors like Francois Truffaut and Jean-Luc Godard famously rebelled against France's entrenched film production system, especially its postwar preoccupation (like Hollywood's) with conservative narrative strategies, including highly plotted dramas and literary adaptations, along with conventional formal strategies dependent upon static, set-bound, carefully lighted shots, and performances by established stars that were often stagey and nonnaturalistic. Against the homogeneity and "false perfection" of the studios' so-called Tradition of Quality, the new filmmakers instead favored what Truffaut called "realism and life."[2] In their attention to authenticity, the filmmakers were influenced by Italian Neorealism's formal preferences, including casts of nonprofessional performers, on-location shooting for both interiors and exteriors, and long-duration, often-mobile, shots made with available light. As Nowell-Smith explains, the benefits included the ability to convey a profound, slice-of-life sense of place: "Getting out into the streets was a way of catching life as it is lived and peripheral things going on in sight of the camera or the characters [that] are often as important as the main action itself."[3] In terms of narrative strategies, they tended to avoid the classical cinema's tightly constructed, plot-driven films in favor of loose narratives with episodic scenes that are not always causally motivated, and open, often less-than-happy endings. Characters are constructed differently too. Unlike studio films, protagonists are not traditional heroes that experience extraordinary triumphs; instead, they tend to be more passive and less goal-driven. As Nowell-Smith explains, in the New Wave films, "the loser acquires a new prominence" and "the traditional hero has no place."[4] Moreover, the films are often self-reflexive about film history by referencing famous and iconic moments from earlier films, including silent era films. Most significantly, each of these strategies is characteristic of shorts that preceded and were contemporaneous with French New Wave features, such as *The 400 Blows* (Truffaut, 1959) and *Breathless* (Godard, 1960). Finally, as Nowell-Smith notes, there was great diversity in their methodologies; as he explains, the European New Waves "did not replace one form of storytelling with another, but with several," which the following analyses aim to demonstrate.[5]

Shorts on the Leading Edge of the New Waves

The Red Balloon is not typically associated with the French New Wave, but it is an early title whose storytelling strategies helped to forge the path and whose extraordinary success was registered on many levels. A legendary fiction short, it arguably is the most significant live-action fiction title from the 1950s. A discussion of *The Red Balloon* heeds the recent call among film scholars for an expanded view of the French New Wave and its films and filmmakers. As Ginette Vincendeau explains: "We urgently need to extend the familiar New Wave corpus to new filmmakers . . . [to] include new film titles, [and] to revise the classic periodization of the New Wave beyond the accepted span of 1959–1963 . . ."[6] The following discussion of *The Red Balloon* is longer and more detailed than others in this volume, in order to demonstrate some of the depth and breadth one may bring to the study and analyses of live-action art shorts. In large part, the analysis foregrounds aesthetic and narrative issues with some attention to critical responses, though it is by no means exhaustive in those areas either.

Written and directed by Albert Lamorisse, the thirty-four-minute *The Red Balloon* is a masterpiece of visual expression and narrative economy, which is suggested by its focus on the relationship, from beginning to end over the course of a few days, of its two principal characters, a little boy and his balloon, with each receiving a fairly equal share of narrative attention. It is also a masterpiece of visual artistry and performance; as film critic Michael Koresky observed, it is "one of the all-time greatest examples of pure cinema."[7] Critics have deemed it a "cinematic landmark," an example of "timeless magic," and "one of the most beloved films of all time."[8] Arguably, *The Red Balloon* is not only an important short film, it's one of the more significant narrative films of any length in cinema history.

Balloon has a simple, well-designed narrative with fewer characters and events, a brief story time, an episodic, chronologically ordered plot, an emphasis on naturalism, and long-duration occasionally mobile shots along with carefully composed static and near-static framings. In addition, *Balloon* uses actual locations, mostly exteriors, emphasizes visual storytelling and performance styles, uses dialogue sparingly, and is self-reflexive about film history. Finally, *Balloon*'s combination of a fictional narrative with elements of surrealist fantasy would be echoed in many later shorts.

Set in Paris, *Balloon* tells the fantastic story of a little boy, Pascal, who discovers a lively red balloon that he manages to tame so that it becomes his companion, until a nasty group of bullies set their sights on destroying it. Pascal's adventures with the balloon begin on his way to school when he discovers it tethered to a light standard. After rescuing it, he goes about his routine, but the balloon repeatedly proves to be a less than welcome presence and the two are rejected several times: when they are not permitted to board the streetcar, and at school when the principal locks Pascal in a small office to punish him for bringing the disruptive balloon. But the ultimate rejection occurs when Pascal goes to church with his mother and a deacon chases them away after the balloon follows them inside. In addition, the balloon elicits increasingly hostile responses, especially when the bullies commence their unrelenting efforts to capture and control it.

In the end, the bullies succeed but lonely Pascal is saved when scores of balloons rush to console him.

Several of *Balloon*'s episodic sequences function more comically than causally, as when Pascal enlists the aid of people with umbrellas to protect the balloon from the rain, and on the occasions when the balloon teases Pascal by dashing out of his reach. Several sequences also provide color and atmosphere, as when Pascal and the balloon wander through a busy flea market and Pascal stops to study a tall painting of a little girl with her own round companion, a hoop, while the balloon pauses in front of a tall mirror. One sequence, in particular, suggests *The Red Balloon*'s slice-of-life sensibility. A brief montage, it serves as the transition between the end of the first day and the start of the second, as it shows a few of the neighborhood's denizens as they attend to their early morning routines: a shopkeeper opening his bakery, a mailman delivering letters to a woman hanging laundry, and a repairman walking up a lovely hill while toting a sheet of glass on his back. The sequence provides a sense of life as really lived in the Ménilmontant neighborhood of Paris and, although it establishes the time of day, it is otherwise causally unmotivated. The loose narrative and episodic organization of *Balloon* proved to be significant in the development of the art short, and also were favored in the French New Wave features that appeared a few years later.

As is common in short films, *Balloon*'s economy is partly the result of the spare characterization and development of its protagonists. Both Pascal and the balloon are presented without exposition, and the boy does not undergo the kind of character change that is conventional in feature-length films. Indeed, until his bully antagonists appear, Pascal's goal is rather diffuse—to remain in possession of the balloon while he goes about his usual routine. One film reviewer commented favorably upon Pascal's limited characterization, saying: "When the film is over, you realize that although you've been entirely enveloped in little Pascal's fantasy world, you've learned next to nothing about the boy himself. . . . With such a skimpy back story the film runs the risk of abstraction, but . . . [all] that matters here are the balloon, the boy (whoever he is) and the steep, narrow streets of Ménilmontant, where they play together."[9]

Visually, *The Red Balloon* combines artistic and documentary-style strategies that feature both moments of sheer contemplative beauty and naturalistic sequences that convey a powerful sense of authenticity (see Figure 5.1). Both its fixed-frame and mobile shots have a compelling naturalism and bring to mind André Bazin's reverence for the power of the photographic image to elevate the real. He might have been talking about *The Red Balloon* when he said: "The aesthetic possibilities of photography reside in the revelation . . . of the real. This reflection in a wet sidewalk, that gesture of a child . . . , only the impassive lens . . . could present it in its virginal purity to my attention, and consequently to my love."[10] With a preference for longer-duration shots, *Balloon* develops a pattern of carefully composed often fixed-frame shots in addition to a few striking mobile shots whose accelerated rhythms add great dynamism and narrative intensity.[11] Shot in

Figure 5.1   *The Red Balloon* (1956)

color and entirely on location by cinematographer Edmond Sechan, *Balloon*'s mise-en-scene is characterized by a generally reduced color palette dominated by a rich range of grays. At times the images are almost monochromatic, but they are neither flat nor free of detail. For example, several wide shots take advantage of the diffused light and the richness of its atmospheric perspective, while other noteworthy details include shots of the often-cloudy sky, the misty Parisian light, the streets and buildings of the neighborhood and vistas beyond, and even Pascal's blue-gray jacket and pants. Addressing the quality of the light in particular, one reviewer said: "In all the films set in the Paris streets, you have ... never seen this light—this glowing painterly dawn that caresses the grayish buildings."[12] Against the reduced palette, the saturated and nearly surreal red of the balloon provides an irresistibly vivid contrast; as one enthusiastic reviewer commented, the "bright gloss of the balloon's curve even outshines the sheen of rain-slicked streets."[13] Another writer, observing the contrast between the gray landscape and the red balloon, read it symbolically: "the Ménilmontant section of Paris ... overwhelmingly gray in its postwar days [is] so expressively melancholy that the appearance of the balloon's blazing-red roundness serves as a nearly angelic counterpoint, a beacon of hope."[14] Although the gray palette remains dominant, in addition to the balloon, there are several bright spots of saturated color, especially in the enchanting sequence when hundreds of multicolored balloons fly through the sky from points throughout Paris to rescue Pascal and lift him out of his despair after the bullies finally destroy his beloved balloon.

The Red Balloon's aesthetic intentions are established immediately with the opening image, which one reviewer praised for its "Cartier-Bresson-like photographic beauty."[15] A wide, fixed-frame shot, it has a keyhole framing and deep space composition that shows a neighborhood street and buildings situated at the top of a steep set of stairs. The misty light suggests the early morning, and the foreground is mostly in silhouette while the background is hazy with a picturesque, cloudy sky. Near the stairway, centered in the frame, a cat sits quietly and into this still moment, from the bottom of the frame, the silhouetted Pascal walks toward the cat, which he pets for a few seconds before descending the staircase. The shot is held for a moment, which enables the contemplation of both the setting and its beauty. In addition to their exquisite pictorial beauty, *Balloon*'s carefully composed still and mobile shots provide a richly detailed portrait of postwar working-class Paris and its busy inhabitants, so the settings are more than backdrops for the film's action—they are very much living environments, which are as compelling as the story and characters. The film's prologue underscores the importance of the setting, as it acknowledges the "assistance of the children of Ménilmontant" and the "balloons of Paris." *Balloon* includes a beautifully crafted self-reflexive shot too, as its framing and figure movements recall one of the earliest and most famous French motion pictures, Auguste and Louis Lumière's single-shot, *Workers Leaving the Factory* (1895). A fixed, wide-angle composition, the shot shows Pascal's classmates as they leave the schoolyard at the end of the day. Like its predecessor, it provides a slightly oblique view of the doorway to the school, which is centered in the frame, just as the large group of happy children quickly exit and disperse.

The Red Balloon is filled with remarkable shots, far too many to discuss; however, the one that depicts the "death" of the balloon merits attention as the film's most emotionally intense. The setting is suggestive: a grim, rubble-strewn, apparently war-pocked field, where Pascal unexpectedly runs into the group of bullies for their final showdown. When the balloon refuses to leave his side, the bullies unleash a slingshot attack and, as Pascal watches helplessly, it slowly loses air and drifts to the ground. The sadness and loneliness of the balloon's demise is both a function of the setting and the period of time devoted to it. Taking place during the film's longest duration take, of sixty-five seconds, it shows the balloon alone in a medium shot as it transforms from spectacularly round, plump, and shiny to dull, wrinkled, and listing until it is fully deflated. The tragedy of its demise is further emphasized as the sequence plays entirely without sound, until one of the bullies delivers the *coup de grace* by stomping the balloon flat.

The performance of Pascal (played by Pascal Lamorisse, the director's five-year-old son) is worth discussing briefly as it reflects one of the most enduring legacies of the silent era on shorts—the entirely dialogue free or, as in *Balloon*, the nearly dialogue-free film.[16] Pascal's performance is a visual one that recalls the physical energy and famously reduced facial expressions of the American silent film comedian Buster Keaton. For almost the entire film, Pascal's face is alert but mostly inexpressive and he does not smile until close to the end when, in one of the film's very few closer shots (a medium close-up), he smiles broadly as he registers his delight at being surrounded by the big bunch of multi-colored balloons. As in silent comedies, the majority of *The Red Balloon*'s action is presented in long and wide shots, so Pascal's broad movements and dynamic, slightly exaggerated, and often-comical poses are easy to read. Also, like his silent comedian predecessors, Pascal spends much of his time running—to and from school and, especially, away from the bullies. Particularly amusing is the slapstick-style sequence that takes place in a series of narrow alleys, where Pascal and his wildly flapping balloon try to elude their determined antagonists and must overcome a series of obstacles—a dog and a slow old woman—that provide both comic and dramatic tension. But the balloon's "performance" is perhaps even more striking than Pascal's. Also conveyed in wide shots, it is magical as it bobs, ducks, and sails alongside Pascal and sometimes on its own.[17] Not surprisingly, several critics were captivated by the believability and timing of the balloon's movements. *The New York Times* praised its comic appeal, noting its "entrances and exits from the frame [are timed] with the precision of a crack farceur."[18] As for the balloon's sad ending, *Entertainment Weekly* declared that the "technical miracle" of the balloon's movements and transformation conveyed "true" feeling: "The thing doesn't merely shrivel—it damn near *emotes*."[19]

The balloon's performance inspired André Bazin to issue high praise for Lamorisse's "creative originality," and to use *The Red Balloon* as evidence of the "virtues" of montage. Key for Bazin was that the balloon's animated movements are shown in longer-duration wide shots and are not due to tricks of editing. In other words, instead of suggesting the balloon's independent movement via a series of separate shots, the balloon's actual movements are shown. For Bazin, the strategy enabled a "reality" effect, in which the preservation of and respect for spatial unity conveyed the illusion of movement convincingly. As he explained: "Lamorisse's red balloon actually does go through the movements in front of the camera that we see on the screen. Of course there is a trick in it, but it is not one that belongs to cinema as such. Illusion is created here . . . out of reality itself. It is something concrete, and does not derive from the potential extensions created by montage." Bazin was so captivated by the "reality" effect that he characterized *The Red Balloon* as "an imaginary documentary."[20]

The Red Balloon's ending, though uplifting and triumphant for Pascal, is nevertheless open, which reflects the art short's preference for narrative ambiguity. It also reflects the short film's penchant for intense endings. The last image is an exquisite wide shot that shows Pascal and the huge collection of balloons floating high above Paris— but into an unknown future. As one critic mused, "I always wondered where he went after the credits rolled," while another noted that the film ends with a "flourish of ambiguous release."[21] *Balloon*'s ambiguities go beyond the ending, however, as its story invites several possible readings. One critic offered the following: "The film can, and has, been read in a number of ways—as a social commentary on post-war France seeking to escape their wartorn cities, a scathing attack on the oppression of individuality and even as a Christian allegory complete with death and resurrection."[22] Using *The Red Balloon* as his reference point, the American director Tim Burton captured the combination of meanings and moods evoked by the image of a balloon: "There's always been something about balloons. . . . You see them deflated and you see them floating. There's something quite beautiful and tragic and sad and buoyant and happy, all at the same time."[23]

Ostensibly a children's film, *Balloon*'s remarkable success demonstrates a much wider and enduring appeal. There has perhaps been some reluctance among scholars to address *Balloon*, due to its general status as a children's film; however, film critics and reviewers since the beginning have embraced it in expansive terms. Upon its release in 1956, *Balloon* earned critical accolades, international festival and theatrical screenings, and several awards, including the Palme d'Or at Cannes. In the United States it became (and remains) the only short film to win the Academy Award for Best Screenplay. It also won a special British Academy of Film and Television Arts Award and was named one of five "Top Foreign Films" by the National Board of Review. After a successful theatrical release in the United States in 1957, it became even more familiar when it was featured in a special prime-time television presentation in 1960.[24] Also, throughout the 1960s, *Balloon* was widely screened in classrooms and other non-theatrical settings in the United States, and it has been credited with being the largest-selling nontheatrical print in American history.[25]

The importance of *The Red Balloon* to short film history and to the emergence and development of the art short cannot be overestimated. Released several years before landmark French New Wave features like *The 400 Blows* and *Breathless*, its widespread circulation likely helped prepare international audiences for the riches of the European art cinema in general. Among other things, its success in the United States demonstrated the viability of short film distribution in the era of post-studio, independent production and helped to provide a kind of "brand recognition" for short films. It also likely contributed to the cinephilia of the generation of filmmakers that came of age in the 1960s. Indeed, Koresky notes its widespread circulation and credits *Balloon* with being, for many young people at the time, "My First Art Movie."[26] Also worth noting is that it made the image of a red balloon an icon for Paris, nearly as familiar as the Eiffel Tower and the Seine, which is a remarkable legacy for a film of any length.

Before considering a few of the shorts made by French filmmakers more typically associated with the French New Wave, it is useful to note the significance of another touchstone title *Two Men and a Wardrobe*, Roman Polanski's legendary, award-winning student film, which is significant both aesthetically and historically (among many other things) and is one of the few fiction shorts familiar to film scholars. It is also productive to consider *Two Men* at this point in the discussion because it conveys the adventurous filmmaking of the early live-action fiction art short and shares some significant similarities with *The Red Balloon*.[27] Film theorist Jean-Pierre Geuens calls *Two Men* "solid as a rock, an undeniable masterpiece, an absolute work of art."[28] Very much like *The Red Balloon*, *Two Men* features outsider protagonists and also combines a simple yet interpretively open narrative and elements of surrealism, with a naturalistic visual style dominated by patterns of long-duration mobile shots. Polanski wrote, directed, and played a small role as a street thug in the black-and-white, fifteen-minute, dialogue-free film, shot entirely on location. A fish-out-of-water tale, *Two Men* features a pair of happy young men who inexplicably emerge from the sea while carrying a full-size wardrobe. As they delight in their arrival on shore, they mug and dance around a bit in silent-comedy fashion, after which they embark upon a sojourn through the local town. As in *The Red Balloon* their odd object is an unwelcome distraction to the authorities and townspeople in a streetcar, a cafe, and a hotel, and as they continue their journey, they endure increasing hostility and violence from the locals—and what they witness is even worse. Polanski said the film's theme concerns the "intolerance and stupidity of society," and he described the story as one in which: "People can't stand the sight of them traipsing around with this thing, especially when they go into cafés or try to get onto a tram. They stick out and because of this provoke hatred wherever they go. I wanted to show the unpleasant things going on in town around the two of them, all these crimes that no one does anything about because everyone's focused on these two strangers."[29] The crimes range from the apparent killing of a cat to the broad-daylight murder of a man. In the end, the two lonely, outcast men and their wardrobe return to the sea and an uncertain future.

Two Men is most certainly a key title in short film history and the development of the art short; and, like *The Red Balloon*, it is inevitably mentioned and highly regarded in reference books. However, in critical and academic discussions of shorts from the mid-to-late 1950s, *Two Men* has received the overwhelming bulk of attention.

Richard Raskin, for example, considers it both a "masterpiece" and "landmark" whose combination of experimental and narrative strategies signified the emergence of the "modern short fiction film," which "combines the cinematic innovation of the experimental film with the telling of a coherent, meaningful and intelligible story."[30] Given that both films share the same basic narrative strategies, with an emphasis on a simple yet open-ended story, told episodically, and feature characters with unusual companions that provoke the ire of their neighbors, along with a shared preference for location shooting and naturalistic visual styles mixed with more fantastic elements, *The Red Balloon* is likely the more significant title in terms of identifying the earlier emergence of the art short.

As for the filmmakers most often associated with the French New Wave, their first films were shorts, including Jacques Rivette's, Francois Truffaut's, and Jean-Luc Godard's. Jacques Rivette's *The Fool's Mate/Le Coup du Berger* (1956) is typically the earliest short referenced in relation to the New Wave, though it seems to be as much for its production and the inspiration provided by its low budget and the spirit of collaboration among friends, including co-screenwriter Claude Chabrol, as for its style and story.[31] Colin MacCabe deems it the first film of the critics-turned-filmmakers "gang," and likely the most collaborative film of the French New Wave.[32] At twenty-eight minutes, it is certainly a longer, more complex short that includes a voiceover prologue that relates the characters in the moral tale to be told to players in a chess match and promises that not only will there be a "fool," it will be the protagonist Claire. Though it is highly amusing and fascinating (and a bit vicious), it is also somewhat less economical and more highly plotted than its New Wave successors, with a cast of several characters and locations. Yet it also is unified by its theme of adultery and features an entirely unexpected twist ending. The story involves a young bourgeois wife (Claire), in the midst of a love affair, who schemes with her paramour to keep the lovely fur coat he's given her, without divulging its source to her husband, though their complicated plan backfires and produces two twists that explain why Claire is the film's "fool." The first reveals the coat's final beneficiary—Claire's sister, and the second reveals that the sister is having her own love affair—with Claire's husband.

Truffaut was inspired by Rivette's production process and *The Fool's Mate*'s success to undertake his first completed film, *Les Mistons/ The Brats* (1957), which is perhaps the most often-cited landmark on the path to the French New Wave revolution. Truffaut scholars Diana Holmes and Robert Ingram have declared it "one of the first shots to be fired in the campaign to launch a new way of making films, the campaign that was to become the Nouvelle Vague. . . ."[33] In 1959, *Film Quarterly*'s reviewer noted the film was part of the long-anticipated body of work from "the crop of rising young French directors" and praised it as Truffaut's "auspicious debut."[34] In addition to many critical accolades, the eighteen-minute *Les Mistons* won the best director award for short film at the Brussels Festival of World Cinema. It also reflects the art short's profound attention to the subject and representation of youth. An adaptation of a short story by Maurice Pons, it tells a dramatic coming-of-age tale punctuated by several moments of levity. It also has a slightly more complex story and organization, and includes voiceover narration.[35] Wheeler Winston Dixon praises *Les Mistons'* spirit, characterizing it as a "short, elegiac, [and] gorgeous" film that "bursts with the energy of summer and youth." Pauline Kael likewise noted its "marvelous command of sensual image and atmosphere. . . ."[36] Shot on location in the provincial town of Nîmes, *Mistons* proceeds episodically as it follows the titular brats—a group of undifferentiated preadolescent boys—who spend their summer idolizing the lovely young woman Bernadette and loathing her lucky boyfriend Gerard. The first shot is an exhilarating long-duration mobile take of Bernadette riding her bicycle along a tree-lined street, which is accompanied by the first-person narration of one of the now-adult brats, as he recalls, rather poetically: "Jouve's sister was unbearably beautiful. She always rode with her skirts flying. Bernadette led us to discover many of our darkly hidden dreams. She awoke in us the springs of luminous sensuality." The brats live up to the film's title by tormenting the young couple relentlessly in the hope it will destroy their romance. Their tortures include stalking the lovers on the street, the tennis court, and the cinema, and extend to sending an erotic postcard to Bernadette to make her suspicious of Gerard. Although the brats themselves fail to spoil the couple's happiness, they soon learn their love story has ended tragically with the death of Gerard in a mountain-climbing accident.

Les Mistons closes with the narrator's last lines that recall the film's first images and its subtle combination of nostalgia and the unrequited longing of youth, which are further underscored by the metaphorical movement into the new Fall season: "But one autumn day in October, Bernadette Jouve passed us, not seeing us. Later I recalled the event more with pity than shame, but I have a bitter memory of her gone from our childhood skies, the way she'd disappear around a corner with her skirts flying." Although *Les Mistons* is a coming-of-age tale, presented from the perspective of an older, wiser adult, and a rather complex one with more characters, situations, and locations, it reflects the art short's tendency to resist sentimentality and facile epiphanies. Instead, it provides a fairly nuanced and carefully modulated view of adolescence that also, like the art short in general, resists tidy, banal, and unambiguous interpretations. Not surprisingly, *Film Quarterly*'s reviewer applauded *Les Mistons'* brevity and depth: "Truffaut has told his story with economy and precision, infusing it with humor, tenderness, and a poetic beauty. . . . His film has more truth and life . . . than many films have in three or four times its length."[37]

Les Mistons is also unabashedly self-reflexive about motion pictures; indeed, it is packed with references to other films. As Richard Neupert observes: "*Les Mistons* repeatedly reminds the viewer it is made by a young man who loves movies and is not afraid to call attention to his world of *cinéphilia*."[38] Most famously, it recreates the legendary gag in the Lumiere brothers' *The Waterer Watered* (1895), when the brats amuse themselves by pulling the same water hose prank on a gardener at the tennis court where Bernadette and Gerard are playing. In addition, the film Bernadette and Gerard are watching at the cinema that inspires them to kiss, and which elicits catcalls from the brats, is Rivette's *Le Coup du Berger* during the moment when the young wife and her lover are kissing in his apartment. It's also note-worthy that each of the self-reflexive moments function mostly as comic diversions (rather than causally), as when the boys pretend to be Hollywood-style gangsters, complete with over-the-top death falls conveyed in forward and reverse slow-motion; and when Gerard asks a funny, bug-eyed man on the street for a light and the man barks, "Jamais!" ("Never!"), which recalls a similar moment in Luis Bunuel's *The Criminal Life of Archibaldo de la Cruz* (1955). Truffaut's determi-nation to make *Les Mistons* an unconventional film, of course, suc-ceeded. As Holmes and Ingram note: "The freshness and spontaneity of *Les Mistons* can be attributed to the fact that it marked, in 1957, a new departure: its setting was contemporary and recognizable as were its characters and themes. It was distinctively French, could not be easily ascribed to any particular genre, and was free of the formu-laic characteristics" of mainstream cinema.[39] Among the film schol-ars to acknowledge the significance of *Les Mistons* to Truffaut's career and to film history in general is Richard Neupert. His monograph *A History of the French New Wave Cinema* is one of the few to address, and in considerable depth, the short films of the New Wave direc-tors, including Francois Truffaut, Jean-Luc Godard, and Eric Rohmer, and to see them as significant aspects of the era's filmmaking. Indeed, Neupert's commitment to the films is suggested by the cover of his book: an image from Truffaut's *Les Mistons* that shows young Gerard and Bernadette kissing.[40]

Comedies are somewhat less common in the art short (and tend to be dry in sensibility) than in the classical short but are perhaps more common than in the feature-length art film. *All Boys are Called Patrick/Charlotte et Véronique* (1959) is Godard's first fiction short, a charming anti-romantic comedy written by fellow *Cahiers du Cinema* critic and French New Wave director Eric Rohmer.[41] Both historically and aesthetically significant in the development of the art short, *Boys* demonstrates the strengths of a compact, episodically arranged narra-tive, and the pleasures of self-reflexivity. Shot on location in Paris, the twenty-one-minute short features two protagonists, the titular friends and roommates, each of whom separately meets the same young man,

Patrick, at the Luxembourg Gardens. Much of the humor depends upon the depiction of Patrick as a bit of a Lothario who uses the same pick-up lines on both young women, who are unaware that they have dates with the same guy. After chatting excitedly about their "separate" Patricks, Charlotte and Véronique go for a walk together and catch the rogue in the midst of seducing yet another young woman. When the two friends realize their mistake, instead of being angry with him or each other, they stroll away together laughing. Like its art short predecessors, *Boys* includes several self-reflexive film references, such as the Elvis Presley and James Dean posters that decorate the women's apartment, the jaunty nondiegetic piano score, and exaggerated figure movements, along with moments of slightly speeded-up motion, which recall the rhythm and style of silent era comedies. There's also an amusing reference to Truffaut, when a café patron is shown reading an issue of the weekly journal *Arts*, whose headline declares, "French Cinema is Collapsing Under False Legends," which is the title of a Truffaut-authored diatribe against the tradition-bound French film industry.[42] Certainly, *Boys* with its simple story, and the casual ease of its comedy—both physical and dialogue-based, and its naturalistic visual style helped to counter those "false legends" and to expand the art short's comedic dimensions.

The Art Short: Since the New Waves

The legacy of the early art shorts is both wide and deep. As the following examples demonstrate, there are many compelling and noteworthy titles that convey the art short's preference for bold, unconventional, or offbeat content, along with tones, often used in combination, that range from light and comedic to dark and dramatic, and styles that range from naturalistic, with a documentary impulse to shoot on location to capture regional specificities, to stylized combinations of live-action cinematography with bits of animation and computer-generated imagery. The following discussion considers the most prominent narrative and thematic registers and modes represented in the art short category since the 1950s, including those that enable the form's concision and unity. Though certain aspects to be addressed may be shared with some feature-length films, the difference concerns their preponderance in the art short. Among the general patterns and preferences germane to and well represented in the art short, in particular, are the following storytelling and narrative strategies: character sketches; coming-of-age stories and representations of children and youths; experimentation with time; representations of fantasy, dream, and surrealism; and representations of social realism and social issues. Finally, as in chapter four (herein), the discussion reflects the significance, especially for narrative containment and unity, of several recurring strategies that enable the short film's economy, including the journey, the single meeting or conversation, and the brief relationship.

As the following examples also suggest, the art short has a tighter range of running times compared to the classical short, so there are fewer examples of shorter shorts. Nevertheless, the art short category is exceptionally varied in its stories, characters, and moods. Further, since the 1960s, the art short has been committed to conveying dimensions of authenticity, even when mixed with fanciful narrative elements, and does so in a variety of ways, including by means of subtle characterization and a detailed attention to location. Before proceeding, it should be noted that the analyses of individual titles in each general category are not organized chronologically or by national cinema and are intended to convey the wide-ranging use of the strategies since the 1950s. The consideration of several individual titles is intended to enable familiarity with a substantial body of compelling, often award-winning, and canon-worthy titles. It also helps to suggest the greater global circulation of short films, which has been enabled by festivals and, more recently, by the Internet. However, it also should be noted that the films discussed below, unfortunately, provide a very limited view of the global array of short film production. And, admittedly, due mostly to availability issues, many non-Western shorts are underrepresented in this survey of art shorts so titles from the United States and Europe are disproportionately represented.

The Character Sketch

Character sketches are not only more common in the short than the feature-length film they are well suited to the brevity of the form. As noted in chapter three (herein), shorts, in general, favor characters that do not undergo change (or do not change dramatically), especially in contrast to characters in feature-length films. Character sketches, in particular, tend to focus on more detailed, multi-dimensional and less stereotypical, yet fairly static, representations of protagonists that reveal them—as in a portrait. In addition, protagonists tend to be less motivated to achieve large-scale goals so they are less active as narrative agents and, more often, function as passive witnesses. The analysis of *About a Girl* (Percival, 2001) in chapter three (herein) is suggestive in that, although the unnamed protagonist has a fairly immediate goal, to dispose of the bag she's carrying in a distant part of the canal, she does not change or develop during the course of the film but is gradually revealed instead.

The legendary Senegalese filmmaker Ousmane Sembene's *Borom Sarret* (1963) is a beautiful example of a character sketch that provides a slice-of-life representation of an unconventional protagonist—an impoverished taxi-cart driver in Dakar, Senegal. An eighteen-minute, black-and-white drama, *Borom Sarret* tells a heartbreaking yet simple story with a documentary sensibility using a journey-oriented narrative. The hard-working cart driver's experience is conveyed in extraordinary depth as he laments, in first-person voiceover, that in his postcolonial "modern life" he is a "working slave," despite that his "forefathers were heroes." Though he continually beseeches God for mercy, the driver's attempts to carry paying passengers to support his young family are beset by challenges, including thieves who steal rides, people begging for charity, missed meals, and a creaky, broken wheel. But his greatest indignity occurs when a well-dressed, prosperous looking man insists, over the cart driver's objections, that he take him out of the "natives' quarter" into the city where carts are forbidden. Upon reaching the city, a policeman stops the driver to issue a fine and confiscate his cart while the rider proves himself a thief by sneaking away without paying. As the driver leads his too-skinny horse back home, he desperately realizes that after another long day's work, he will return to his wife and family penniless once again and acutely aware of the economic disparity and other injustices that distinguish his family's life from the lives of more privileged families in the city. In addition to its deeply affecting portrait of the taxi driver, whose experiences are depicted not so much as life changing but as more routine travails, *Borom*'s slice-of-life sketch and dramatic intensity are enabled by its simple chronological organization. Finally, its depth and authenticity might seem to belie *Borom*'s brevity, but its careful attention to regional specificity and location are integral to the characterization of the taxi driver and to conveying the larger context of economic inequality.

Gowanus, Brooklyn (Fleck, 2004) is a more recent film (from the United States) that continues the legacy of the 1950s art short in its attention to naturalism and subtle characterization, with a twenty-minute running time and chronological, episodic organization that enable a carefully detailed portrait of its protagonist. Winner of the "Best Short" Award at Sundance, *Gowanus* was shot on video and has a raw yet beautiful visual style with a pattern of mobile, often long-duration shots made, or so it seems, with available light. Set in the hard-scrabble, working-class neighborhood of Gowanus, it provides a delicate character study of Drey, a reserved twelve-year-old who is sweet, strong, and also a mostly quiet observer. She is introduced in an arresting and mesmerizing close-up, facing the camera, almost looking into it, with a sucker in her mouth. Despite her youth, which is emphasized in the opening shot, Drey has some serious issues in her life, including a harried and loving single mother, a brother who spends most of his time on the street, and a teacher with a bad habit. When Drey discovers her teacher hiding in the girls' bathroom smoking crack after school one day, she responds in her usually reserved way, but still unexpectedly, by asking for a ride home. Although there is an undercurrent of tension later about what she might do with her newfound knowledge, Drey is nevertheless drawn to the often-brusque teacher and seems sympathetic to his apparent loneliness—at one point offering him one of her suckers. Several sequences add fine detail to the characterization of Drey and her closest relationships, including moments between Drey and her mother, whose exchanges are alternately angry and loving; and a riveting and seemingly unscripted sequence that underscores the sharp contrast between Drey and her girlfriends, when she quietly listens as they pontificate about boys and romance. Perhaps most compelling is Drey's observation of her teacher's awkward lecture about Hegelian opposites and the notion that "we can only know the essence and not the appearance of reality," which might be as profound as it is self-serving. As is often the case in character sketches, the depiction of Drey recalls the "lonely characters" typical of short storytelling (discussed in chapter three [herein]), and the film's visual style helps to make the point, as it's dominated by shots and sequences that show her alone, by way of single shots and character placement, even when she's with others. An especially captivating episode shows Drey skating leisurely through the neighborhood without an apparent final destination, stopping to watch the river, and skating next to the massive wall of the elevated train, which makes her seem even smaller and more alone. *Gowanus*'s last shot is as remarkable as the first: It shows Drey, in another single shot, but this time in the foreground of a wide, deep-space, shallow-focus composition with a blurry Statue of Liberty in the background, as she blows a gum bubble. It not only underscores *Gowanus*'s commitment to providing a slice-of-life sketch of its protagonist, rather than a character whose "arc" involves profound change, it also demonstrates the art short's persistent refusal to provide easy understanding, familiar scenarios, or characters with clearly defined goals. Indeed, that refusal is suggested by the symmetry of the opening and closing shots, both of which emphasize Drey's youth—sucking on a lollipop in the first, she's blowing a bubble in the last.

The fifteen-minute Australian drama *Cracker Bag* (2003) was written and directed by Glendyn Ivin and won several festival awards, including the Palme d'Or at Cannes. A slice-of-life story set in the early 1980s, it features a ritual occasion and another lonely protagonist, a

rich naturalistic visual style and a quiet, measured rhythm of longer-duration shots, including several close shots that capture colorful period details. Told episodically and without much dialogue, its
unsentimental character sketch concerns a working-class suburban
girl, nine-year-old Eddie, who is seriously committed to her effort
to collect as many "crackers," or fireworks, as she can for her celebration of "Cracker Night."[43] In addition to arguing with and tattling
on her brother to their single mother, the less-than-charming Eddie
sells the soda and beer cans that she sneakily weights with pebbles for
the money she uses to buy fireworks. She also spends time lovingly
arranging and admiring them, before storing them in the homemade
canvas bag that gives the film its title. On the big night, Eddie carefully lights her first firework, a rocket, but she unknowingly knocks
it over, which causes it to sail into and ignite the big bunch of fireworks in her bag so they detonate all at once. Utterly stricken, she
hides her face in her mother's chest and misses the spectacular beauty
of the display, though her brother and mother are awed by it. *Cracker
Bag*'s last sequence is subtle and ambiguous, as it shows a tear-stained
Eddie sitting alone in the backseat during the drive home. Distracted
by the offscreen sound of fireworks hissing, she recalls (in a quick
flashback) the moment when the rocket landed in her bag, and then
watches from the open car window as a lone firework explodes in
the sky. When it's over, she very briefly looks directly into the camera
with the slightest hint of an enigmatic smile, which echoes and is as
open to interpretation as the film's opening shot, which introduces
Eddie while she gazes into the camera. One critic, speaking to *Cracker
Bag*'s perhaps more universal appeal, said that part of its power is to
"remind us of the moments in our lives when we failed to grasp that
one perfect thing."[44]

For other strong examples of character sketches, see the Appendix
entries for *Pourvu Qu'on Ait L'Ivresse . . .* , a French short from 1958 by
Jean-Daniel Pollet about a lonely young man hoping to find a dance
partner at a local dance hall; *Five Feet High and Rising* (Sollett, 1999),
an award-winning student short set in downtown New York City,
which is also a coming-of-age story about its boastful and irresistible

yet naïve twelve-year-old Victor; *Trevor* (Rajski, 1994), a rare comedy-musical art short whose over-the-top visual style matches its charming adolescent protagonist, Trevor, who's mad about the divine Diana Ross and is facing some early questions about his sexuality; *Robbie* (Harvey, 2012), a science-fiction title that features a lonely sentient robot who's been circling in space for decades without companions; and the compelling Romanian short *Traffic/Trafic* (Mitulescu, 2004), whose protagonist is ostensibly on a journey to an important work meeting; though he never gets there, his brief stops and encounters along the way, including with his daughter, provide a portrait of a detached and ambivalent urban professional whose most intimate conversation is with a stranger.

Youth Appeal

Motion pictures have long been attentive to representing children and youth onscreen, especially in feature-length films; but, arguably, the art short, which is also oriented to representations of youths, does so with much greater variety and nuance. And, as noted above, the preference for challenging depictions goes back to *Zero for Conduct* and is matched by its New Wave inheritors, *The Red Balloon*, *Les Mistons*, and *All Boys are Called Patrick*. More recently, the character sketches *About a Girl*, *Gowanus, Brooklyn*, and *Cracker Bag* suggest the enduring fascination with detailed and naturalistic representations of children and youths in live-action fiction shorts. The Palme d'Or winner and Academy Award nominee *Skaterdater* (Black, 1965) is an historically significant youth-centered film that brings a documentary sensibility to its focus on the subculture of skateboarding. Considered the first-ever film of any length to feature the then-new sport, it is entirely dialogue-free and energetic in its use of a mobile camera, longer-duration shots, and an upbeat instrumental surf music score. *Skaterdater* is also a coming-of-age tale. Shot on location in coastal suburban Los Angeles using nonprofessional performers, who were real-life competitive skateboarders, its eighteen-minute, episodic narrative offers a parable about adolescence, peer pressure, and the first stirrings—and challenges—of young love. The protagonist is a pre-teen boy who's the leader of a group of skateboarding buddies and whose leadership and loyalty are tested when he becomes attracted to a cute local girl. When his buddies discover his romantic preoccupations, it leads to a climactic duel that pits the protagonist against his nemesis teammate in a skateboarding duel that involves a harrow-ingly high hill, which is made more exciting with some action-film strategies, including rapid and cleverly elliptical editing. When the boy loses the duel, he gets the girl, but both his and his former team-mates' futures remain uncertain at the end.[45]

Two Cars, One Night (2003) is a more recent coming-of-age art short that captures the power of the passing moment. An Academy Award nominee from New Zealand, it was written and directed by Taiki Waititi, who noted in the film's press kit that he wanted to fea-ture a moment in which "an unexpected joy is found in the every-day, a moment of beauty in the ordinary."[46] A twelve-minute-long dry comedy, with a very spare narrative and clever dialogue, it uses a single location and lush, high contrast black-and-white cinematogra-phy for its semi-autobiographical story of a chance meeting that leads to a brief relationship (see Figure 5.2). One night, as two brothers in one car and a girl alone in another wait outside a rural pub for their

Figure 5.2 *Two Cars, One Night* (2003)

parents, the eldest boy, who's nine, proves to be a chatty sort who amuses himself by insulting the eleven-year-old girl in the next car when he catches her eye with "poetic" witticisms such as, "Oi ugly. Hey girl. Oi, ugly girl." But she has her own way with insults, so the intrigued boy eventually joins her in her car. The two kids engage in some teasing and boasting as they get to know each other, and their attraction is capped when the girl gives the boy her costume-jewelry "diamond" ring just as her father returns to the car. The film's open ending is slightly downbeat as it shows the boy quietly watching as she drives away. Although it's conversationally based and uses a fixed setting, *Two Cars* has a remarkable visual dynamism due to an inventive use of cinematography, editing, and rhythm, including the several angles and focal lengths that provide varied views of the car and the pub, in addition to time-lapse sequences, shifts between closer and wider shots—both still and mobile, and a carefully modulated alternation between slower and quicker shots and editing rhythms. Furthermore, the cast of characters consists entirely of nonprofessionals, which lends a sense of authenticity to their relationship as it moves from nasty, awkward, and playful, to heartfelt—though with an unclear future.

For additional examples of child- and youth-oriented (and young adult) art shorts, see the Appendix entries for *The Bakery Girl of Monceau/La Boulangere de Monceau* (Rohmer, 1962), the French director's first "morality tale" about a fickle young man's romantic quest; *Asad* (Buckley, 2012) about a Somali boy in the midst of political tumult who longs to be a fisherman or a pirate (like his friends); *The Earrings* (Mamatkulova, 2010), a beautiful short from Kyrgyzstan that features the first meeting and early attraction and developing love between a young man and woman, who seem destined for a happy marriage; *Bean Cake* (Greenspan, 2001) about a fish out of water in a new school who loves bean cakes more than anything else, which brings serious trouble on his first day; *Six Dollar Fifty Man* (Albiston and Sutherland, 2009), a New Zealand period drama that features a fearless, determined, often-bullied, and odd little boy with a fascination for the 1970s television hero "The Six

Million Dollar Man"; and the *Buzkashi Boys* (French, 2012) a searing naturalistic drama set in Kabul about two boys with a fascination for the national sport of buzkashi, which is a variation on polo played with a dead goat. In addition to the titles recommended above, as character sketches, *Five Feet High and Rising* and *Trevor* also feature youths.

Time Play

As noted in chapter three (herein), the importance of the "unity of impression" in the art short is often indicated by the emphasis on carefully selected moments and fragments of time. Although it's unsurprising, since it's a defining feature of the form, the short fiction film is frequently fascinated with time, which is reflected in the preference for elliptical narratives and a more general experimentation with time. The preoccupation with brief moments, and the frequency of episodic narratives underscores the significance of ellipses to the short's spare stories. The literary theorist Allan Pasco has observed that the short story form so depends upon ellipsis that, "[r]eaders expect to generalize, to read in depth between the lines."[47] The short film's bold experimentation with time and the frequency of spare, elliptical narratives are suggested by the art shorts, *Wind/Szel* (Ivány, 1996) and *With Raised Hands/Z Podniesionymi Rekami* (Panov, 1991), both of which were inspired by well-known and historically significant black-and-white still photographs. *Wind* is a Hungarian short based on Lucien Hervé's photograph, "Les Trois Dames," and was a Palme d'Or winner at Cannes. A black-and-white film with no dialogue, it unfolds in a single long-duration circular pan shot that lasts six minutes as the slice-of-life imagery goes from innocuous to harrowing. The shot begins with an image that matches the source photograph, in which three middle-aged women stand expressionless and evenly spaced in a line in front of what appears to be a house while they gaze at something offscreen. As the pan begins, it cheats expectations that what the women are seeing will immediately be shown because the camera moves slowly in the opposite direction, and with a consistent speed for the duration of the film. At first, the shot reveals a placid and beautiful rural landscape until the moment that a group of men watching something offscreen appear, and then a single dead man hanging from a post appears, which is followed by the revelation of several other hanged men. Finally, the full scope of what the women have been watching is revealed—a shocking and inexplicable tableau that shows several men standing amongst several tall wooden posts on which dead men with cloth sacks over their heads have been executed by hanging while another man is being readied for hanging. When the camera reaches the point at which the shot begins, the still-expressionless women slowly turn to go into the building behind them and the source photograph, "Les Trois Dames," appears. The intensity of the ending is due to the surprising scene it finally reveals, the length and measured pace of its single suspenseful shot, and its profound ambiguity about how and why this awful scene has transpired.

With Raised Hands is a Polish film that, like *Wind*, won the Palme d'Or at Cannes and was shot in black and white without dialogue. It was inspired by a photograph made by an anonymous photographer in the Warsaw ghetto during the Second World War that depicts a group of Jewish prisoners in street clothing surrounded by armed soldiers, in the foreground of which is the heartbreaking image of a little boy standing with both of his hands raised as though in response to a demand. With a six-minute running time, *With Raised Hands* is a highly elliptical film that, although it consists of several shots, seems to depict a brief and continuous stretch of time. The slice of life it reveals is, also like *Wind*, shocking. But, in this film, there's a temporary moment of respite. *Hands* begins with a tight shot of a motion picture camera being prepared for a shot, which is followed by a point-of-view shot from the photographer's perspective as he adjusts focus and frames his image of, at first, a medium close-up of one of the soldiers who smiles as he comes into focus. Then, in the same point-of-view shot, several prisoners are ordered by aggressive soldiers to assemble and, as the photographer shifts to a wide lens, the image begins to match the source photograph as one soldier grabs a little boy and forces him to face the camera with his arms and hands raised. Subsequent shots show the prisoners—men, women, boys, and girls—as they appear through the photographer's lens until, unexpectedly, the wind blows the little boy's hat off of his head and out of the frame. While the soldiers and photographer are apparently distracted, the boy drops his hands and sneaks away, though precisely how he does so is elided. Next, a sequence of shots show the boy chasing his wind-blown hat and finally saving it, intercut with shots from his point of view as he briefly watches while the tragedy he's escaped is still being photographed. In another elliptical moment, the boy seems to make a full getaway behind a wall so he is no longer visible, though, in the film's last shot, he tosses his cap into the air twice in an apparently celebratory gesture. The final image adds considerably to the film's intense ending, as it shows the source photograph. Addressing the significance of the elided moments in which the boy escapes first from the view of the soldiers and then from the view of the audience, the director Mitko Panov said: "I am generally a great fan of film lapses. I like films in which more is hinted than told. . . . they don't spell everything out for you . . . Before that moment [when the boy tosses his hat] there is another lapse, when the boy actually escapes from the sight of the photographer. We never see that critical moment of the boy running around the corner. We just see that he is no longer there." For Panov, the ending addresses a universal theme but remains open; as he explained, the film is about "the desire to be free, whatever that means."[48]

The short film's facility for exploring unorthodox representations of time includes some compelling variations that provide profound access to character subjectivity and unique experiences of time. The legendary French short, *An Occurrence at Owl Creek Bridge* (Enrico, 1962), Chris Marker's science-fiction masterpiece *La Jetée/The Pier* (1963), and the more recent award-winning *Bullet in the Brain* (von Ancken, 2000) each turn on their protagonists' subjective experiences at the precise moments of their deaths. In the first case, a man hung for a Civil War crime experiences a fantasy in which he does not die but returns home to his wife, which we see from his perspective as though his fantasy is reality. Of course, the legendary and often-discussed science-fiction short, or more precisely, the avant-garde "photo-roman," *La Jetée*, is Marker's sublime, elegiac portrait of a man caught in a brutal dystopia. *La Jetée* has a rich, complex narrative constructed from exquisitely composed high-contrast black-and-white still photographs, with the exception of one brief moment of motion, all of which is made dynamic with carefully modulated editing rhythms and a precise attention to spatial continuity. Told without dialogue, except for some indecipherable whispering, it uses omniscient voiceover narration that provides access to the protagonist's thoughts and experiences. *La Jetée* takes place in a grim post-nuclear future, whose leaders are experimenting with time travel without success until they discover that the protagonist, a prisoner, who's haunted by a tragic memory from his childhood, might be a perfect guinea pig. From its use of still photographs, to its complex time-shifting organization, *La Jetée* is overwhelmingly preoccupied with time and the thematic exploration of the relationship between time and memory, which underscores the resonance of particular moments (and images) from the past.

Bullet in the Brain is a dramatic art short that provides great depth in its access to the subjectivity of a dying man, and turns on the beauty of a spontaneous, ephemeral, exquisite, and seemingly insignificant moment from a childhood baseball game that provides a happy epiphany during the man's last moments. Written and directed by David von Ancken, *Bullet* is a loose adaptation of the Tobias Wolff short story and has a fifteen-minute running time. The protagonist, Anders, is in many ways an ugly man who craves beauty. A dispirited university writing teacher, he is shown in his classroom berating his students mercilessly about their lack of talent and sharing his own interest in the carefully chosen words that can recreate a moment. As he winds down his harangue, he asks one of the students, "Do you believe in the chance that you could be changed by something as timid as a word? . . . The chance at salvation from the rational?" After class, on a trip to the bank, Anders is angry again when a pair of robbers burst in with blazing aggression. When one of the robbers, apparently unknowingly, quotes lines from famous gangster tales,

Anders, an enemy of cliché, cannot help but laugh, which leads to the fulfillment of the title's promise as the robber shoots him. It is at that point that the film's omniscient narrator takes over.

After an experimental sequence that poetically evokes what happens as the bullet tears through his brain, the voiceover recounts the memories that are also enacted for the viewer in montage, but which Anders himself does not recall, memories that include what would ordinarily seem to be one's most indelible—experiences with a girlfriend, his wife, and his daughter. What Anders remembers instead is a long-forgotten moment from his childhood, when he was on a baseball field and a fellow player declared that shortstop is "the best position they is." Although forgotten until his dying seconds, Anders remembers the grammatically incorrect phrase as perfect; as the voiceover reveals, he found himself "strangely roused, elated, by those final two words, their pure unexpectedness and their music" (see Figure 5.3). The transcendence of the words for Anders is underscored by the dreamy, golden-hued imagery and ambient sounds used to depict that gentle and singular summer day. With an intricately constructed narrative organization and a combination of visual styles—both naturalistic and stylized—*Bullet* moves between the present and the past and between reality and memory to give an astonishingly expansive

Figure 5.3   *Bullet in the Brain* (2000)

view of the protagonist's life during his final moments. It is unusual for a short (or any film) to provide access to a character's interiority in the way that *Bullet* does and to do so with such precision and economy. Both Anders's impending death and realization, finally, of his longed-for perfect words enable the film's emotional and psychological resonance, and its unity. It also illustrates the power and depth of a well-chosen moment and evokes Nadine Gordimer's observation that short storytellers "see by the light of the flash; theirs is the art of the only thing one can be sure of—the present moment."[49]

Fantasy/Surrealism/Dream versus Reality

Although fantasy, surrealism, and the dream, and the sometimes blurry lines between those modes and reality, are not unknown in the classical live-action fiction short, such narrative elements tend to be more common in the art short and they are a significant legacy of the European New Wave shorts, including *The Red Balloon* and *Two Men and a Wardrobe* and, the legendary French New Wave precursor, *Zero for Conduct*. Although it's not typically included in the French New Wave, Georges Franju's art thriller *La Première Nuit* (1958) is nevertheless a significant and instructive French title; it won the Grand Prix at the Mannheim Film Festival in Germany and is also noteworthy for being shot on location by the legendary German cinematographer Eugen Shufftan. Like *The Red Balloon* and *Two Men and a Wardrobe*, *Nuit* includes elements of fantasy and surrealism, which are cued by the prologue that suggests the importance of fantasy in our daily lives. *Nuit* also adds a beguiling play with the lines between real and unreal, waking life and the dream to the art film's repertoire. With eerily beautiful imagery and a languid pace, the twenty-minute *Nuit* has a spare story, told entirely without dialogue, that combines a bittersweet coming-of-age tale with the myth of Orpheus and Eurydice. The protagonist is an apparently lonely boy who becomes enchanted by a girl he sees and follows in the Metro, where he inexplicably spends the night. While asleep on an escalator, the boy dreams he sees the girl or her apparition several times in the deserted station, and sometimes it seems the girl does not see the boy but, on a few occasions, she looks at and smiles at him. However, the two never actually meet. The most visually arresting sequence occurs when the boy boards an empty train that departs the station and, at one point, his train's car and the one carrying the girl become aligned as they temporarily travel in the same direction. For several seconds, the two youngsters gaze at each other and she smiles very slightly until their trains diverge, and the boy registers the impact of her loss with a falling tear. *Nuit* then ends ambiguously when the boy awakens and leaves the urban Metro station, and a dissolve provides the transition to a series of wide shots of the boy walking alongside a creek on a lonely country road. *Nuit*'s unity in its depiction of attraction, longing, loss, and loneliness is both dreamy and melancholy, and rich with possible meanings.

Hungarian filmmaker István Szabó's fascinating Academy-Award nominated student film *Koncert* (1962) is a sixteen-minute dialogue-free art short shot on the banks of the Danube that has eccentric moments of surreality and touches of silent-style visual comedy. In addition, *Koncert*'s visual style includes dynamic black-and-white cinematography and a pattern of long-duration, mostly wide, mobile shots, and a few eccentric shots that use extreme angles and odd imagery. Like *The Red Balloon* and *Two Men and a Wardrobe*, *Koncert*'s narrative is dominated by a curious object, a piano sitting atop a bike cart, which is introduced as three men transport it alongside the river. The trio stop to play the piano, which produces both amused and annoyed responses from people nearby. But soon, the men are distracted by another odd object, a large mirror with an elaborate frame that reflects topsy-turvy images of buildings and sky as it moves along. At first, it's unclear how the mirror is being moved, until the pretty young woman carrying it comes into view, whereupon the enchanted trio abandons the piano to follow the mirror. But the piano does not remain alone for long, as several people with varied talents play it, much to the delight of onlookers. *Koncert*'s other offbeat moments include a long-duration tracking shot made from the opposite bank of the river that follows a composer who runs a great distance until he reaches the piano, and displaces a talented player in order to play the piano himself; a large and fancy portrait that suddenly and inexplicably appears propped atop the piano; a man with his arm in a complicated cast that forces his arm into a gesture that looks very much like a Nazi salute; and the vicious rainstorm that suddenly erupts and sends everyone scurrying for protection, until a few brave souls rush back to protect the piano with their jackets. The ending provides some symmetry with the opening, as another trio of men ride into the distance with the piano, and the original trio returns, running madly with arms akimbo until the closing freeze-frame. *Koncert* presents a continuous stretch of time and series of incidents and has a carefully designed narrative, but it's a loose, spare, and elusive one. That is, although one can identify a theme regarding the power of music, its meanings are open to interpretation.

The offbeat Swedish film *World of Glory* (1991), written and directed by Roy Andersson, is among the even more interpretively open and elusive shorts and offers absurd, inexplicable moments that test the line between reality and illusion. *World* presents a series of episodic tableaux, whose content and tones range from harrowing to darkly comic, and which are made with long-duration, wide-angle, fixed-frame shots, and a reduced, cool, and almost monochromatic palette. The opening sequence is the darkest, though it seems to promise darker things to come; it shows a young girl being loaded, with considerable resistance on her part, into a panel truck already full of naked prisoners. After the door is closed, a man connects one end of a large hose to the truck's exhaust pipe and the other to the van's interior, thus ensuring that the victims inside will be gassed to death with carbon monoxide. Occasionally a witness of sorts is present during the episodes, though his presence is neither explained nor referenced even when he looks into the camera. Each of the subsequent episodes (which are separated by a black screen that lasts for a few seconds) features a middle-aged real estate broker as he appears in different settings and in a usually calm, direct address to the camera, as he introduces his family members one by one, including his dead father—by way of his tombstone. The other sequences provide some additional yet very slight characterization as they show the broker in his bathtub, at the barber's, a shoe shop and, in an oddly amusing yet also disturbing sequence, on the floor of a crowded restaurant where he's become inexplicably entangled in his suit jacket so that he cannot see and despite his cries for help, none of the patrons respond. Usually the broker is positioned precisely in the center of the frame, though the pattern is broken a few times but without a clear reason why. Along the way, he addresses several issues, including the difficulty young people have purchasing apartments, and the "necessity" of securing a sponsorship to nurture his son's tennis "gift," with the help of a logo being tattooed onto the boy's forehead by the man who acts as a witness in other episodes (see Figure 5.4). The last two sequences show the protagonist at church taking communion and drinking too much sacramental wine, to the consternation of the priest, and then in his bedroom as he covers his ears and explains that he thinks he hears screaming. As the film progresses, it becomes clear that the title is ironic, but the film's possible meanings remain largely open, though one can discern a theme that concerns the act of being a passive witness or, perhaps, the willful "inability" to see or hear the

Figure 5.4   *World of Glory* (1991)

large and small cruelties that humans enact against each other, which recalls *Two Men and a Wardrobe*. For additional examples of the play with fantasy/surrealism and reality, see the Appendix for *The Man Without a Head/L'Homme Sans Tête* (Solanas, 2003), a fanciful title in which a man prepares for a much-anticipated date by hoping to replace his missing head; *Me The Terrible* (Decker, 2012), a delightful and inventive, yet also dark, portrait of the adventures of a fearless pirate girl on a journey to conquer New York City and its most identifiable locations, which uses a combination of live-action and other imagery; and *Zapping* (Mungiu, 2000), a dour and oddly surreal exploration of the absurdities of life for a working-class television addict in modern Romania.

Social Realism/Social Issues

As several of the discussions above suggest, attention to naturalistic depictions and authentic slices of life also are well suited to often bold and challenging representations and explorations of social conditions and social issues. In particular, *About a Girl* and *Borom Sarret* are among the art shorts that feature careful portraits of their protagonists and also reveal much about the social and economic realities of their lives and environments. Far more than the classical short, and perhaps more than feature-length films, the art short has a high proportion of titles that explore social circumstances and issues and do so with a wide range of strategies and tones, from provocative but softer-edged shorts like *The Lunch Date*, to shatteringly naturalistic and sometimes grim shorts like *Wasp*.

The Lunch Date (Davidson, 1990) is an eleven-minute student film that won several awards, including the Palme d'Or and the Academy Award, and which offers a more gentle exploration of the routine racism—and comeuppance—of its privileged, elderly protagonist. Set in New York City's Grand Central Station, it uses dialogue very sparingly and deploys striking high-contrast black-and-white cinematography that favors longer-duration shots (see Figure 5.5). The opening sequence is dynamic as it features images of the busy

Figure 5.5   *The Lunch Date* (1989)

station at rush hour, which are compelling for their spontaneity and seamless integration—and unscripted interactions—between the actors and real-life passersby. The compact story concerns a chance encounter between a well-heeled, fur-clad middle-aged white woman and a homeless black man, which takes place after the woman, apparently heading home after a shopping excursion, misses her train. That she's likely a racist is quickly established when she bumps into a well-dressed black man and drops her handbag, spilling everything inside; as the man stops to help her retrieve the items, she rudely insists that he "please don't touch them" and proceeds to blame him for delaying her. When she just misses her train, she stops at a station diner for a quick bite and, after purchasing a salad, she leaves her bags and food in a booth while she goes for a fork. But when she returns to her seat, she discovers a homeless black man not only sitting in the booth but also enjoying her salad. Although she insists that it's "my salad," the man silently continues eating and, miffed, she begins eating it too. When he leaves and returns with two coffees, she begins to soften a bit and almost smiles. In the end, the film's twist is revealed: on the way to the train, the woman realizes she's left her bags behind and returns to the diner, only to discover that her own salad has been waiting for her all along—in another booth—and she has been mistaken about the man too—he's no thief but rather a kindly and generous gentleman. Apparently realizing that she's another victim of her own preconceptions, she laughs and heads for the train. Although *Date*'s ending is somewhat less open, its attention to character, detail, location, and rich cinematography are significant characteristics in the art short.

Wasp (Arnold, 2003) is a searing family drama shot on location, using a pattern of hand-held long-duration shots that provide a documentary-style sense of authenticity further enhanced by naturalistic performances, which won the Academy Award and several festival awards. A fascinating, beautifully acted and directed—and also relentlessly dark—British short, *Wasp*'s protagonist is an angry twenty-three-year-old single welfare mom with four hungry young daughters. When she leaves them on their own outside a pub while she's inside pretending to be childless for the sake of an old school acquaintance, hours go by and the girls grow even hungrier and more listless. The title refers to the wasp that finds its way into the baby's mouth after the eldest girl, in desperation, feeds her some discarded spareribs to stop her crying. Despite that the mother's parenting skills are rather less than ideal, much of the twenty-four-minute-long film's power is due to the refusal to judge her as it provides a slice-of-life view of her life and circumstances, and refuses to provide easy meanings.[50] For additional titles, see the Appendix for *Victoria Para Chino* (Fukunaga, 2004), a gripping account of the tragic journey a group of Mexican immigrants makes to Texas; *Illusions* (Dash, 1982), an exploration of studio era Hollywood and the limited opportunities for African-American women; *In the Morning* (Lurie, 2005), a true-life story about the rape of a Turkish girl and its aftermath; *New Boy* (Green, 2007), an Irish short that alternates between lighter and more harrowing moments to touch on the difficulties of an African boy who has left his homeland in the wake of a family tragedy and finds himself the only black pupil in his new school; and for a comedic and satiric consideration of the struggles of the American family farmer against the rapacious banks and farming corporations, see *The Accountant* (McKinnon, 2001).

Of course, the analyses of each of these live-action art shorts could go much further, with attention to their many interpretive possibilities, as well as to aspects of their production, distribution, and exhibition, among many other things. In addition, although the list of titles provides a sense of the development and the scope of the art short, along with some familiarity with several landmark and otherwise noteworthy titles, it is, by necessity, limited. A fuller sense of the scope of both the classical and art short is provided by many of the titles included in the Appendix.

Before closing, I wish to add that this sojourn was inspired by my first encounters with shorts, as a professional, during my work as a film programmer; I've never thought of shorts as the "little brother" to the more valued feature-length film and my high expectations about them were and continue to be rewarded, as both a cinephile and scholar. Thus, I share the sentiments of another short film enthusiast, the movie critic Richard Brody, who uses a compelling set of analogies to make the case for the importance of the short to the larger field of film culture (and I would include, academia):

> The short film doesn't supplant the feature; it nourishes it. It doesn't make a filmmaker's career, but it augments it, just as a brief visit to a friend may bring a wise word that may stick with a person for a lifetime. Or, to put it another way, movie theatres are like restaurants, which offer a chance for a good long talk; but there are also cafes for a chat, and the cinema needs those too.[51]

Appendix

7:35 in the Morning (Vigalondo, 2003, 8 minutes)

An Academy Award–nominated Spanish short that parodies the convention of integrated musicals in which performers are inspired by the spirit of life to break into song and dance. The setting is a café where people in the midst of their morning routines are interrupted by the lead performer who unexpectedly begins to sing and dance. Soon, he is joined by the other café patrons, whom he has apparently forced to sing lines and dance steps. During the performance, the leader reveals that he's a terrorist who is loaded with explosives, and the film ends with a shock when a woman who is not part of the "performance" secretly calls the police and the terrorist is apparently killed as the offscreen sounds of gunfire suggest. *7:35* uses black-and-white cinematography more evocative of the documentary than the musical, and its suspense is enabled by the odd and unpredictable combination of terror and dark comedy.

The Accountant (McKinnon, 2001, 39 minutes)

An Academy Award winner, *The Accountant* is a longer short with a complex, darkly comic narrative that includes several characters, locations, and a longer-story duration. At its center is a low-key and offbeat freelancer, whose methods are both unorthodox and illegal but apparently helpful to those in dire financial straits. Summoned to help a seriously indebted and depressed farmer with a cheating wife, the accountant advises him to burn his buildings and "accidentally" lose several of his limbs in order to collect a pile of insurance money. In the end, the farmer comes up with another plan that's even more drastic, but it saves his family and the farm. Along the way, *The Accountant* makes some timely and acerbic political points about the brutality of banks and corporate farming and their disastrous effects on family farms.

Amblin' (Spielberg, 1970, 26 minutes)

Spielberg's first 35 mm film, with a spare, earnest, and dialogue-free story features some poetic landscape imagery that evokes the Western in its tale of a young "pioneer" on a journey to the Pacific. While roaming the desert with his guitar case, a young man meets a fellow wanderer, a young woman, while hitchhiking and they begin traveling together. Their journey is punctuated by hitchhiking, drugs, sex (apparently), an odd olive-pit-spitting contest (that seems intended to evoke silent era comedy), and ends when they reach the beach in Malibu. While the protagonist delights in splashing in the water's edge, the young woman looks through his guitar case, takes a few items, and then unceremoniously walks away, presumably out of the young man's life forever.

Asad (Buckley, 2012, 16 minutes)

An Academy Award nominee, *Asad* has a somewhat complex narrative given its running time. It is about a Somali boy, Asad, introduced at the shore as several boys are heading off to their work as pirates. Unhappy because he's too young to go along, Asad agrees to carry a giant fish to the village for an old fisherman. When Asad sees his friend being threatened at gunpoint by some vicious, heavily armed men on the hunt for women, he saves him by giving the men the fish. Upon returning to the shore, Asad finds the fisherman injured, apparently by the same armed men, so he's unable to go out fishing. Though he's never caught anything, Asad insists upon taking the boat out on his own to make up for the loss of the old man's fish. Instead of catching any fish, he soon spots a yacht, goes aboard, and finds the tragic aftermath of the boys' piracy. He also discovers a small, fluffy white dog, which he rescues, much to the delight of the fisherman and his village friends who believe his tale of catching a "lion fish." In addition to an unadorned, naturalistic visual style, a particular strength of the film is its nuanced characterization of Asad, who is very much a kid despite his composure when he encounters brutality and other terrors.

The Bakery Girl of Monceau/La Boulangere de Monceau (Rohmer, 1962, 24 minutes)

The first of the French New Wave director's "moral tales," *Bakery Girl*'s protagonist is a rather unlikable young man (played by Barbet Schroeder) who becomes preoccupied with two women. Among its many visual and storytelling pleasures are the specificity of its Parisian locations, a pattern of fluid mobile shots, a quick rhythm, and a simple story built upon repetition and coincidence. When the young man twice crosses paths with a pretty young woman on the street, he obsessively prowls the neighborhood for her without luck. After a few unsuccessful days, he meets a second young woman—the "bakery girl"—and visits her shop several times to flirt with her while he purchases ever-increasing amounts of pastry. She responds favorably to his attention, but he proves fickle once again when he ditches the bakery girl after unexpectedly running into the first young woman for a third time.

Bean Cake (Greenspan, 2001, 13 minutes)

A Palme d'Or winner and USC thesis film, shot in beautiful high contrast black and white, *Bean Cake* is an art short set in Japan about a quiet, sensitive rural boy on his first day at a new school. Very much a fish out of water, he is immediately taunted for being a "country bumpkin" without a proper uniform. Even worse, he makes the mistake of looking at the kindly class leader rather than the teacher, which provokes the angry teacher to ask what he likes best in the world. When the boy answers "bean cakes" and not "the emperor," the enraged teacher issues a cruel punishment by forcing him to sit outside in a less-than-comfortable position until he properly answers the question. The boy finally gives in, hours later, when his stricken mother arrives. In the last scene, the boy and sweet class leader are at his house, where she tries his mother's bean cakes and declares them "delicious." But when she asks, "Do you like the bean cakes better than me?" the film ends with the boy apparently in another no-win situation.

Before Dawn (Kenyeres, 2005, 13 minutes)

A Hungarian art short that screened in competition at Cannes, *Before Dawn* has a very elusive, dialogue-free, continuous-time story conveyed in only a few long-duration, languidly panning wide shots. Opening on a vast grassy landscape, a lone van appears and stops. When the van's horn sounds, a group of illegal workers or immigrants who have been hiding nearby in the grass suddenly stand up and board the van. Almost immediately the van is intercepted by a phalanx of military-style vehicles, including a helicopter, and the people are quickly arrested and hauled away.

When the camera pans across the now-empty landscape, a lone man who's been hidden in the grass unexpectedly stands up, looks around with a startled expression, and walks away. In keeping with its enigmatic narrative, *Before Dawn*'s ending is open, as it's unclear how the lone man came to be there or why. Was he meant to be part of the unfortunate group that boarded the van? Was he asleep during the dramatic events? Or, is it something else entirely?

Big Business (Horne, 1929, 18 minutes)

One of the Hal Roach studio's successful Laurel and Hardy series shorts, *Big Business* was selected for the National Film Registry and is a strong example of the continuing popularity of silent slapstick shorts, though it was made during the early period of the sound era. Shot on location with an unadorned style, its story is slim and has the comedy pair trying to sell Christmas trees by going door to door. Of course, they encounter and invite many tribulations, which begin when they fail to heed a homeowner's "no peddlers" sign and he responds with a hammer blow to Oliver's head. But when they ring one doorbell too many times, a series of gags ensues as the hapless salesmen do battle with the homeowner in a tit-for-tat of escalating acts of violence and mayhem that end only when the house and the duo's Christmas tree truck are destroyed.

Black Rider/Schwarzfahrer (Danquart, 1993, 12 minutes)

The Oscar winner *Black Rider* is a wry German comedy that features a short journey and a charged exchange between two strangers. With rich black-and-white cinematography, it opens with a catalog of quick shots of a busy city and its diverse collection of commuters during morning rush hour. When a young black man finds himself seated next to a terribly racist and insistent elderly white woman on the streetcar, he (and the other passengers) silently endure her increasingly bitter complaints about "savages living off us." When no one objects, it seems to fuel her abusive diatribe. The film's surprise ending and the double meaning of the title (*schwarzfahrer* means both "black rider" and "fare cheat") are revealed when the young man enacts a bit of well-deserved revenge and humiliation by eating the woman's ticket just as the conductor arrives, which ensures a more peaceful journey for everyone when she's thrown off the streetcar.

Blue of the Night (Pearce, 1933, 16 minutes)

A musical comedy, *Blue* is a Mack Sennett production that stars Bing Crosby who plays himself and sings three full songs. Shot simply and basically, it's a light situation-style comedy that features a case of mistaken identity and well-timed coincidences. After his farewell appearance at a nightclub, where he easily elicits swoons from his female fans, Crosby is headed for the train when he accidentally bumps into a young woman, Marion. Coincidentally, they find themselves seated next to each other and as they chat during the journey, Marion claims to be engaged to Crosby, and he plays along to the point of singing another song, which Marion thinks is coming from the radio. In the next scene, at a pool party, Marion's upscale friends discover that she's "engaged" to Crosby, which rankles a nerdy young aristocrat who believes he's her true fiancé. When Crosby unexpectedly arrives, he calms the aristocrat's nerves by convincing the disbelieving crowd that he really is the crooner by singing the film's title song, "Blue of the Night."

Bottle Rocket (Anderson, 1994, 13 minutes)

An offbeat gangster genre short with a dry sense of humor, *Rocket* suggests the continuing legacy of the European New Waves in its episodic organization, location shooting, long-duration, mostly mobile black-and-white cinematography, and self-reflexivity about popular culture. It also suggests the short's preference for judiciously chosen genre conventions. During the course of a few days, two apparently unemployed twenty-something buddies, who behave more like pre-teen boys, undertake the planning and rehearsal for their first heist. When they aren't arguing about the heist, they also chat about *Starsky and Hutch* and, in a sequence that echoes *Taxi Driver*, buy a few guns from a good-old-boy gun dealer. The heist is never shown, their take is only a few dollars, but the exultant thieves extend the afterglow by recounting the details of their triumph over burgers at a local stand. Their future as gangsters is uncertain, however, as the next day they're aimlessly killing time racing each other to the mailbox.

The Bread and Alley/Nan va Koutcheh (Kiarostami, 1970, 11 minutes)

A charming early short from Iranian auteur Kiarostami, *The Bread and Alley* features an amusing, naturalistic slice-of-life moment, conveyed in a pattern of long-duration mobile shots. At the center of its spare narrative is a very young boy carrying bread on his way home and amusing himself by kicking a can down the street. As he tries to pass a big barking dog, who seems more curious than threatening, the boy gets scared and tosses him a bit of bread, which guarantees the dog will follow him all the way home. After the still-nervous boy goes inside, the dog lies down to relax until his next "victim" arrives, which doesn't take long. The film ends when a new boy, this time carrying a bowl of food, arrives in the alley and a freeze-frame captures his worried expression.

Buzkashi Boys (French, 2012, 28 minutes)

An Academy Award nominee, *Buzkashi* is an art short with a gritty documentary visual style that takes place in the busy streets and markets of Kabul, Afghanistan, and on the outskirts of the city, where grim battle-worn abandoned buildings contrast with a breathtaking mountain landscape. An earnest coming-of-age story, *Buzkashi* is about two best friends preoccupied with the national sport of buzkashi—polo played with a dead goat. One boy is homeless and scrappy in his efforts to make a meager living and has giant dreams of becoming a buzkashi champion. The other boy is unhappily apprenticed to his stern blacksmith father and resigned to his already-decided future. But mostly, the two are just boys who want to spend their time playing and exploring. Sadly, when the homeless boy shows his friend the beautiful horse he's stolen to practice for buzkashi, he tries to ride like the champions he idolizes but the horse gallops away with predictably sad results.

Cargo (Howling and Ramke, 2013, 8 minutes)

An Australian zombie-horror art short with no dialogue, *Cargo* is a harrowing, moody story about a man who awakens in a car with a bloody gash on his arm, to find his white-eyed, vicious zombie wife is grabbing at him. The terror of his ordeal is emphasized by a disorienting series of blurry, fragmented shots, with odd angles and quick editing; however, a still bigger horror is revealed—that he has a baby girl. Before he transforms into a zombie, he manages to carry his daughter—the title's "cargo"—on his back and out of his own dangerous reach to safety. After his eyes have gone white, he's shot and killed, but a woman discovers the baby near his body, realizes what he's done to protect her, and gathers her for safekeeping, even if it's only temporary.

The Chicken/Le Poulet (Berri, 1965, 15 minutes)

An Oscar winner, *The Chicken* is a legendary French comedy with a whimsical sensibility that emphasizes visuals rather than dialogue and a charming countryside setting. *The Chicken's* protagonist is a sweet little boy devoted to his rooster and determined to keep him safely away from the dinner table. The boy tries to convince his parents the rooster is really a chicken that will pay egg dividends if its life is spared, and his ruse includes carefully placing eggs under the rooster each night. Not surprisingly, the rooster and his characteristic crowing botches the boy's larger plan but tickles his parents so, in the end, his plan to save his beloved pet succeeds. Along the way, there are several silent-style comedy sequences and musical accompaniments, which are enhanced by some clever fast-paced editing.

Cold and Dry/Tørt og kjølig
(Joner, 2008, 12 minutes)

An offbeat Norwegian art short with a darkly comic sensibility, and a months-long story duration. The protagonist is introduced as he explains a freeze-drying technique meant for people with severe problems that might be solved in the future. After proving successful with terminally ill and mentally disturbed criminals, the technique is now being used by the old and depressed. But when a promotional video convinces consumers that it will give "us all hope," the streets empty of the life that made them vibrant and appealing, until no one is left except the protagonist and a lone cow. The film's visual humor includes its depiction of the progression from life-filled to empty streets, especially as conveyed from the protagonist's point of view.

Daddy's Girl (Allan, 2001, 10 minutes)

The winner of a Jury Prize at Cannes, *Girl* is a naturalistic British short with a dark story about a seven-year-old girl, Teenie, who's introduced alone and trembling in the rain while she waits in front of a pub for her father. During her lengthy wait, she encounters some scary situations including a big dog, a drunken old man who pays her for a kiss, and two bullying boys who taunt her and steal a coin she's found in the rainy gutter. When a young woman runs to intervene, the boys get away, but the Samaritan comforts Teenie, replaces the "ten pounds" the boys stole, and then proceeds to berate her drunken, surly father when he finally emerges from the pub. Undaunted, the father pockets Teenie's cash and the two walk happily away in the pounding rain. But, before they round the street corner, Teenie reveals the film's twist that she really is "daddy's girl," when she waves but follows it with a nasty gesture that bemuses the hapless good Samaritan.

De Tripas, Corazón (Urrutia, 1996, 16 minutes)

A Mexican comedy nominated for an Academy Award, *De Tripas, Corazón*'s protagonist, Martin (played by Gael Garcia Bernal), is a shy young, sex-preoccupied but inexperienced, rural milkman introduced while he's delivering milk to a beautiful young woman with seductive, partially exposed breasts. Captivated, Martin spies on her when she goes to work at the local brothel. When his rougher, sexually experienced friends go to the brothel to indulge their sexual appetites one night, they leave Martin behind. But the next day, he is unexpectedly seduced by the young prostitute, which makes for a happy, sexy coming-of-age ending for young Martin. *De Tripas*' beautiful imagery includes carefully choreographed and composed shots and fluid camera movements.

The Discipline of DE (Van Sant, 1982, 13 minutes)

A lush black-and-white adaptation of a story by William S. Burroughs that provides a meditation on the various ways that one can approach daily life with a "Do Easy" perspective, which includes attention to cool and efficient movements in routine tasks and relaxation. The protagonist is a retired colonel whose life is described in voiceover narration as he uses his DE philosophy to go about his alternately banal and amusing chores, which are then emulated by a young man with much less efficient movements until he too becomes a "student of DE" and it changes his life. His lesson culminates during an "old Western quick-draw gunfight," when he discovers the answer to the voiceover's paradoxical question, "How fast can you take your time kid?"

Dog Years (Hearn and Penfold, 2004, 4 minutes)

An irresistible shorter short shot on one continuous roll of 8 mm film without further editing, *Dog Years* is about a sweet elderly dog, Ben, and his guardian who are spending the day at the beach walking, running, and playing fetch. The shots are cleverly linked by means of the voiceover narration delivered by Ben that describes his life, which is mostly mundane and lonely as he waits the long sad hours for his guardian's return. In a moment of considerable tension, Ben gets dangerously stranded in the water, but his guardian rushes to the rescue to save him and there's a happy ending.

The Earrings (Mamatkulova, 2010, 15 minutes)

Written, directed, and edited by Nargiza Mamatkulova, *The Earrings* is a coming-of-age tale from Kyrgyzstan that delicately renders the love that begins to blossom between two young people of marriageable age. Visually beautiful with lush, colorful wide shots and carefully composed closer shots, it provides a captivating slice of life. *The Earrings* uses dialogue sparingly to tell the story of the unexpected arrival of a woman and her son at the home of a friend and her daughter. The purpose of the visit is to introduce the two young people to one another in the hopes that they might develop an attraction that will lead to marriage. When the mother of the young man leaves her son to help with house chores, the two work well together and exchange several silent, shy, sweet glances but no words. As the day goes on, however, they begin to hold their gazes until, in the end, the young man leaves a pair of earrings for the young woman, which makes his hopes for a future together clear.

Eating Out (Sletaune, 1993, 7 minutes)

Eating Out is a Norwegian dark comedy with a spare, continuous-time narrative and little dialogue that takes place in a single setting—an especially grimy and apparently freezing greasy spoon. The cinematography is simple, mostly fixed longer-duration shots, and the palette is dominated by gray. Despite the unappetizing surroundings, including a seriously grubby cook, a young man in a hooded parka waits for his cheeseburger. As he begins eating, with the manners of a fine dining patron, a pair of inept Bonnie-and-Clyde-style bandits burst in. But while the male bandit demands money, which there can't be very much of in such a dive, his hungry moll eyeballs the still-calm protagonist's burger and orders one for herself. In the end, she sticks around for her meal, and what looks like the beginning of a date, while her shabby bandit ex-boyfriend escapes.

Eight (Daldry, 1998, 13 minutes)

British director Daldry's first film, *Eight* is an art short with beautiful cinematography and an episodic narrative with a nonlinear organization. *Eight* provides a sketch, both amusing and poignant, of eight-year-old Jonathan who is very preoccupied with soccer and who describes himself in the voiceover narration and by way of some direct address to the camera. When he isn't watching and re-watching a favorite soccer match on videotape and re-creating it at the beach with his friend, Jonathan spends his time alone. Eventually a twist is revealed as he explains that his father died before he was born, and Jonathan's apparent loneliness and love for soccer is given another dimension as he recounts that his father passed away at a soccer match, "not playing . . . just watching." The film ends with the boy alone at the beach very quietly singing the song, "You'll Never Walk Alone."

Electronic Labyrinth THX 1138 4EB (Lucas, 1967, 16 minutes)

George Lucas's legendary USC thesis film *Labyrinth* is a canonical title that won First Prize at the National Film Festival and is one of the few post–silent era live-action fiction shorts on the National Film Registry. The style is bold and the story is very simple—and evokes Aldous Huxley's *Brave New World*—in its focus on a man who spends almost the entire duration of the film running to escape his highly monitored science-fiction hell, while a mostly offscreen but always audible team of technology drones try to maintain their video surveillance of him. As he runs, the tension about whether he'll manage to escape is underscored by a hectic editing rhythm, an alternating pattern of odd, often claustrophobic framings and wider shots, and the contrast between video-screen imagery and film footage. As he nears the end of his successful escape, only his side of the "chase" is shown, though the unsettling voices of his video pursuers continue relentlessly.

Epilogue (Allen, 2013, 17 minutes)

A parody of action heroes in which a superhero guy and his sexy cohort/
girlfriend find themselves facing the end of another epic adventure that has
involved getting the magical object that saves the day, so their job is done.
Coming down is hard for the sullen and moody hero, and he can't convince
his boss to give him his next big assignment, which he'd like sooner rather
than later: "What about General Leon? Next Thursday!?" Looking for trouble, he keeps drawing his gun to no avail. Worse, he and his girl are finding
themselves incompatible, since he's longing for world-saving adventures and
she'd rather "take some time off from running and destroying things and killing people." So, they're mostly bored in their Lincoln Towncar and crummy
motel, which leads to arguments and problematic lovemaking.

An Exercise in Discipline: Peel (Campion, 1982, 9 minutes)

Written and directed by Jane Campion, *Peel* is a well-known short that won
the Palme d'Or at Cannes in 1986. The dysfunctional family at the offbeat
center of what a title card indicates is "A True Story" with "A True Family"
consists of an adult brother and sister, Tim and Katie, on a car trip with Tim's
son Ben. The focus is upon the temporary and also absurd duel that develops
between father and son when Ben throws bits of his orange peel onto the
side of a litter-filled road, whereupon Tim stops to insist, irrationally and
viciously, that Ben pick them up, while Katie watches with apparent confusion. Things further devolve when father and son join forces to demand that
Katie retrieve the orange peels that she also has thrown onto the road. The
film's striking and stylized visuals include several extreme close-ups, along
with deep-space shots that show the individual characters arranged so that
they cannot see each other, which helps to underscore their distance and
unstable power relationships.

Fear, Little Hunter/La Peur, Petit Chasseur (Achard, 2004, 9 minutes)

Winner of the Grand Prix at Clermont-Ferrand, *Fear* is a chilling and highly
enigmatic French art short with a slice-of-life narrative. It consists entirely of
one fixed-frame wide shot that shows the corner of a rural house, its scraggly

garden, a chained dog, and a boy sitting with his head buried in his arms in the foreground. The boy calls to his mother a few times and when she appears, she hangs laundry but ignores him. When a ringing sound and yell issue from the house, she runs inside and an unsettling and chaotic bunch of layered sounds, including shouts, screams, crashing, and a train, crescendo to a terrifying pitch. The boy listens and when it stops, he slowly returns to the position he was in at the film's beginning and the mother returns to continue hanging the laundry.

Five Feet High and Rising (Sollett, 1999, 29 minutes)

Rising is a highly regarded New York University student art short that screened successfully and won several awards at festivals, including Clermont-Ferrand, Cannes, and Sundance. Shot on location in New York City's Lower East Side, *Rising* has a naturalistic sensibility in its attention to the specificity of its locations, the authenticity of its performances, and its visual style, which is dominated by documentary-style, long-duration mobile shots. The protagonist is Victor Vargas, a twelve-year-old boy in the midst of learning about the attractions and frustrations of early adolescence. Confident, or at least trying to look that way, Victor undertakes a journey to find the captivating girl he's met at the local public pool, whose ease, self-assurance, and height far surpass his. *Rising*'s extraordinary spontaneity is enabled by several incidental episodic moments, including a high-octane baby bully expending his excess energy, a collection of girls who chat and philosophize about boys and relationships, and several interludes that show the pleasures of kissing. A remarkably long-duration shot near the end captures the strength of the performances in a seemingly unscripted chat between Victor and the girl and the not-a-kid-anymore kiss they share.

Fool's Mate/Le Coup du Berger (Rivette, 1956, 28 minutes)

One of the earliest shorts from a French New Wave director, Jacques Rivette's *Fool's* was also co-written by Claude Chabrol. It has a more complex, less economical narrative (with a longer running time), but is unified in its focus on a young woman at the center of a love triangle. Interestingly, however, *Fool's* falls closer to the classical end of the short film spectrum than the art short end, as it is more plot- than character-oriented and its meanings are largely unambiguous. The protagonist is Claire, a bored young wife, who's having a successful affair with Claude. Claire is the titular "fool," whose indiscretions are compared (by Rivette's voiceover) to a chess game in which it is revealed at the start that she will be the loser. When boyfriend Claude gives Claire a lovely fur coat, they concoct a complicated scheme to hide the fact that it came from her lover. But the scheme backfires and instead of getting the coat back, Claire discovers, by way of the twist ending, that she's positioned herself to be the "fool."

Frankenweenie (Burton, 1984, 30 minutes)

A well-known comedy homage to Universal studio's horror adaptation of *Frankenstein*, *Frankenweenie* was shot in rich, beautiful black and white and has a complex, carefully designed narrative. It tells the tale of a sweet suburban boy, Victor Frankenstein, who makes home movies that star his beloved dog Sparky. After Sparky accidentally gets killed by a car, Victor brings him back to life with some electrical gizmos. Although Sparky seems his old rambunctious self, things go awry when the neighbors become frightened and determine to destroy him vigilante-style by burning him alive. Their mean plan unintentionally injures Victor, but Sparky saves the unconscious boy by dragging him to safety—but the effort does him in and he dies for the second time. There's a happy ending as the contrite neighbors turn saviors and bring the little monster back to life, again.

Franz Kafka's It's a Wonderful Life (Capaldi, 1994, 23 minutes)

An Academy Award co-winner, *Franz* is a Scottish comic parody of, as the title indicates, the dark moodiness of Kafka and the earnest loving family in Frank Capra's Christmas classic. In addition to Expressionist sets that amusingly exaggerate the grim claustrophobia of Kafka's apartment building and his room, the performances are also wildly over the top. The protagonist is the dour, tightly wound author, who's having great difficulty with his new book *The Metamorphosis*. Its absurdly comic situations include moments that convey Kafka's subjectivity when he imagines the sorts of beasts his novel's protagonist Gregor Samsa will awaken as, and when a poor beetle is smashed to death before it can provide the inspiration he needs. Although the title references the Capra film, the story does not; however, Kafka's excessive emoting recalls James Stewart's histrionics in *It's a Wonderful Life*, as does its tidy ending in which everyone comes together for a warm, happy Christmas celebration— Kafka and his new friends, the cheerful and very noisy family downstairs.

Freheit (Lucas, 1966, 3 minutes)

An early student effort, *Freheit* is a brief meditation on freedom, as its German title suggests. The very rudimentary narrative concerns a young man trying to escape from East Germany into West Germany by crossing an impossibly small but treacherous space. While running (in slow motion) with everything he's got, he's shot by guards, which is shown in a few quick, fragmented shots. Though he tries to drag himself the rest of the way, his efforts end badly. As the credits run, over a few still shots of the young man's body, a nondiegetic succession of voices issue platitudes about the importance of the "struggle for freedom," which provides an unexpected level of irony.

Gasman (Ramsay, 1998, 15 minutes)

A Jury Prize winner at Cannes, *Gasman* is one of several excellent art shorts made by the highly regarded Scottish filmmaker Lynne Ramsay. Its subtle story is largely presented from the perspective of a little girl, Lynne, who is introduced in a series of loosely composed, fragmented shots in her working class home, as she happily dresses for an outing with her father and brother while a Christmas tune quietly plays on the radio. After walking some distance, they arrive at a spot on the train tracks where a mother and her two children are waiting for them. Slowly, it becomes clear that Lynne's father has two families, each with a daughter and son, who are meeting each other for the first time. Their destination is a Christmas party where initially wary Lynne becomes friends with her half-sister, who looks more like her twin sister. The film's many strengths include its quiet rhythms and beautiful cinematography, the narrative refusal to judge the father, and the thoughtful, unsentimental representation of the children.

Gossip (Foy, 1929, 20 minutes)

A Vitaphone "Varieties" short based on a play by Lawrence Grattan, *Gossip* is a sketch-oriented comedy of manners with amusing dialogue, characters, and performances, and a well-chosen subject for a dialogue-based short.

It opens with a married couple arguing about a book titled *The Gossipy Sex* and about whom the author means, men or women. The wife is convinced men are the biggest culprits and the husband, of course, insists the opposite. When their mutual friend, Frank, arrives and dominates the conversation with gossip, the wife seems to be winning the argument. Things get amusingly more complicated when Frank gets each of them alone and proceeds to gossip about the absent party. Near the end, when confronted, Frank admits the error of his ways, but when he gets a gossipy phone call, he dives right back in.

The Heart of the World (Maddin, 2000, 6 minutes)

One of several shorts commissioned by the Toronto International Film Festival to celebrate its twenty-fifth edition, *Heart* is Winnipeg auteur Guy Maddin's critically praised and hilarious spot-on parody of Soviet montage cinema, whose black-and-white imagery and frenetic editing beautifully mimic its silent era inspiration. However, instead of a collective "hero" in the Soviet style, its futuristic scenario concerns an heroic protagonist, the beautiful young scientist Anna, who's at the troubled center of a love triangle with two brothers, a mortician and an actor. There's yet another troubled center, the titular heart of the world, which Anna discovers is only a day away from its last beat. As the world descends into chaos, the brothers vie for Anna's love, and she becomes distracted from her struggle to mend the heart by a third suitor—an industrialist. Ultimately, Anna saves the world by devising a provocative scheme that both spoofs the convention of the dramatic climax and suggests the Earth's heart was suffering more from a lack of erotic passion than a lack of love.

Hollywood Bound (Foy, 1928, 9 minutes)

A Vitaphone Varieties comedy short, in which a store clerk, Elmer Frisby, in Iowa believes he's won a contest whose prize is a contract in Hollywood. As he prepares to quit his job and leave everything behind, he gets very full of himself and lords his expectations about his future success over everyone, though they remain highly skeptical. When Elmer appears in a grand living room with a grand woman, it seems he's achieved his dream—especially when she boldly tries to seduce him and he asks her if she's got "it," which was slang for sex appeal. As they begin to kiss the woman's husband interrupts them, whereupon the twist that he's been dreaming while a barber grooms him is revealed. In the end, it's the barber who's headed to Hollywood. In an amusing bit of direct address Elmer declares he's going anyway, and the last shot shows him "cleaning up" in Hollywood—as a street cleaner.

I Love Sarah Jane (Susser, 2007, 15 minutes)

Sarah Jane is an Australian zombie-horror art short that puts a romantic coming-of-age spin on a chilling scenario. In a grim postapocalyptic subur-ban neighborhood, where it seems there are no human adults, a few nasty boys amuse themselves by torturing a lumbering and snarling zombie. Unlike the nasty kids, the protagonist is a quiet boy who's more interested in the sad, angry teenager Sarah Jane. When she catches a bully in the midst of abusing the zombie, who turns out to be her father, she intervenes, which enables her father to scratch his tormentor. And when the bully immedi-ately transforms into a zombie, she delivers some violent revenge by way of a few shovel blows to the bully's head, which only strengthens the smit-ten boy's love for her. *Sarah Jane*'s gloomy story is complemented by fluid mobile shots that reveal an astonishingly detailed rubble-strewn and chaotic landscape.

Ice Cream (Szekely [aka Louis C.K.], 1993, 13 minutes)

An offbeat and very dry comedy with low-key performances, *Ice Cream* has a long story duration and seems to be inspired by David Lynch's characters and stories. Told episodically, with substantial elisions of time that add to the unexpected and amusing series of events, it's about a young couple that goes from first meeting to unhappy family life several years later. Things do not bode well for the two when the young woman's father insists, on their first date, that they marry before having sex. When they have a baby, the new father deadpans, "We shouldn't do that again." Thereafter, the couple tries several ways to ditch the kid, including by leaving it on a doorstop and permitting a magician to make it disappear, but he always ends up back with them, though it's unclear how. The ending is both over-the-top and under-played, as it shows the family together in front of a shop eating ice cream while the boy rides a mechanical bunny, which he continues to do even after his parents are killed when a car smashes into them and a mariachi band shows up and plays a song.

Illusions (Dash, 1982, 34 minutes)

A well-known short that has received substantial critical attention and praise for its subtle and complex exploration of black female identity, *Illusions* is a period film set in 1942 Hollywood. The protagonist is Mignon Dupree, a light-skinned black woman who passes as white, which has enabled her to advance to the executive suites of a movie studio. But when Mignon befriends Ester, a black woman hired to dub the voice of a white movie star, she realizes the irony of her executive position and her role in enabling Hollywood's illusions, which function to maintain the invisibility of black women and to diminish their lives.

In God We Trust (Reitman, 2001, 17 minutes)

Inspired by the 1991 feature-length comedy *Defending Your Life* (Brooks), it won several festival awards and has an upbeat comedic style. The simple narrative concerns a young man introduced as he studies a quarter he's apparently found on the street (which explains the film's title), until he gets hit by a car and finds himself in a way station to the afterlife, where he learns he's headed to hell for his many indiscretions. Panicked, he escapes and lands back on Earth where he frantically tries to rectify his many misdeeds, while encountering some seemingly impossible situations, including a live electrical wire, a gang of bad guys, and a boombox playing "My Vida Loca." In the end, with a final act of charity that takes him back to the quarter in the street, he manages to tip the balance in his favor and reverse his final destination.

In the Morning (Lurie, 2005, 10 minutes)

Based on a true story, *Morning* is a social issue film with an episodic organization that tells a chilling yet simple story. It begins in darkness as a sixteen-year-old Turkish girl walking alone is accosted and then brutally raped by a single attacker. After two months, a group of men meet to decide how to respond to the horrific act, and their discussion is intercut with quick flashbacks to the rape. The ending involves a perhaps anticipated twist in which her brother plays a part in the response to the crime, and an epilogue underscores the frequency of the situation portrayed. *Morning* is a powerful and beautifully shot film, which is punctuated and made more compelling by reminders of the rape conveyed in flashback.

. . . *Is It the Design on the Wrapper?*
(Sheridan, 1997, 8 minutes)

A Palme d'Or winner at Cannes, *Design* is an art short with an eccentric sensibility that concerns a little girl, about six, introduced while explaining that her mother has forbidden her to cross the street alone. The film shifts between the present and the past as the girl addresses the camera to recount the time she was stuck on a street corner and became an easy target for a chirpy market researcher conducting a survey about bubble gum. *Wrapper* combines comedic exaggeration with an undercurrent of darkness, especially the girl's direct address that plays out against a grim backdrop that includes litter-strewn working-class urban settings, her continually annoyed mother, and her parents' offscreen arguments. When the researcher asks her a series of inane questions (like the title's), the understandably put-upon girl takes control by complaining loudly and energetically about the injustices of her young life, which draws the attention of concerned passersby and seems to empower her so that she crosses the street alone and triumphantly.

It's Not Just You, Murray! (Scorsese, 1964, 15 minutes)

Martin Scorsese's well-known student film *Murray* is an ambitious genre-blending comedy art short that won a festival award in San Francisco and was honored at the National Student Film Festival. Shot on location in New York City's Little Italy, it combines and parodies gangster and musical conventions in its portrait of Murray, a middle-aged, mid-level gangster who's very proud of his success; as he explains, in direct address: "I'm very rich and very influential and very well liked." But he's perhaps more proud of his long-term relationship with his best friend, Joe. *Murray* turns on a comic irony, in which what Murray says about Joe's loyalty in the foreground is revealed to be false by what Joe's doing in the background—including his seduction of Murray's wife. As Murray nostalgically recalls his rise from bootlegger to racketeer, his journey to the American dream includes low points, such as jail time and on-the-job injuries, and high points, like the production of a Busby Berkeley–style stage show. Despite its short running time, *Murray* has a complex story and structure that includes flashbacks and several locations.

Je T'Aime John Wayne (MacDonald, 2001, 10 minutes)

Both a loving and carefully crafted homage to and parody of Jean-Luc Godard's French New Wave classic *Breathless*, *John Wayne* features a Jean-Paul Belmondo wannabe who sports his hero's attire, swagger, quick-fire dialogue, tiny apartment—and Lucky cigarettes. To complete the picture, he needs a Jean Seberg-style young woman to romance, and he finds her at the cinema while seeing a French film. With a joyful attention to the imagery and rhythms of *Breathless*, *John Wayne* also features the mobile camera and black-and-white cinematography of its predecessor, which makes the city of London look delightfully Parisian.

Judgement/Simpan (Park, 1999, 26 minutes)

Judgement is written and directed by the South Korean auteur most famous for *Oldboy* (2003). A well-designed short with a wild-ride narrative, it's a genre-blender that combines comedy, suspense, horror, and melodrama with a claustrophobic and stage-like morgue setting, an ensemble cast of characters, and a short story duration yet complex organization that includes actual documentary footage of an earthquake's devastating aftermath. The odd contrast between the documentary sequences and the macabre yet farcical exchanges between the characters in the morgue underscores the narrative's general unpredictability. *Judgement*'s darkly comic sensibility is suggested by the assortment of characters, including an undertaker, a reporter, the body of a young woman killed in the earthquake, a middle-aged husband and wife claiming to be her parents who might actually be pretenders hoping to collect a government death payment, and a latecomer—another young woman who accuses the couple of being her own real but abusive parents. The conflicts between the self-interested characters lead to an outcome of explosive proportions underscored by the shift from black-and-white to color film stock.

Kaal (de Betak, 1996, 14 minutes)

A captivating drama set in India that is earnest but unsentimental, *Kaal* is an art short about an elderly cobbler whose pride is conveyed by the care and diligence of his daily work and his apparent joy in providing such an important service, always wordlessly. With beautiful compositions and rich black-and-white imagery, *Kaal*'s documentary-style attention to detail includes the cobbler repairing, polishing, and arranging the many shoes entrusted to him, and training the young boy who works as his apprentice. When the cobbler becomes too ill to work, the sadness is conveyed by poignant images of his workbox, left alone in the street as the days pass. At the film's end, it becomes clear that the cobbler has died when the boy shows up, opens the old cobbler's workbox, and begins working, with the same pride and diligence as his mentor.

Kitchen Sink (Maclean, 1989, 13 minutes)

A well-known horror art short that played in competition at Cannes, *Kitchen Sink* is one of New Zealand's landmark and most often-cited titles. Relentlessly creepy and claustrophobic in its domestic setting, it begins with a woman pulling a strand of hair from the drainpipe in her sink. The tiny creature that eventually emerges transforms, with her help, into a fully grown man, with whom the woman develops a silent and ambivalent relationship that veers between attraction and repulsion. Its dark tone and visuals are enhanced with painful close-ups, a visceral use of sound, and horror-movie music that accompanies a night of apparent lovemaking between the woman and her Frankenstein. But like Mary Shelley's story, things end badly for the sad creature.

The Lift (Zemeckis, 1972, 8 minutes)

A USC student film, *The Lift* is a black-and-white dialogue-free horror short with a spare narrative about a fancy old elevator (in downtown Los Angeles's Bradbury Building) that seems to have a mind of its own. The protagonist is an office worker who lives a precise and ordered modern life dependent upon a wide assortment of smoothly operating household and office machines, gadgets, and modern conveniences; but the elevator he tries to take each day is a sinister old machine with a gothic sensibility that plays a game of cat and mouse with the increasingly unnerved man until he has a heart attack and dies while racing up the stairs to catch the evil elevator. *The Lift* uses lighting and mise en scene to emphasize the contrast between the man's bright, clean, efficient work and home life and the murderous elevator's shadowy low-key domain, along with a quick editing rhythm that conveys the efficiency of the man's daily routine as well as the increasingly tense duel between the man and the lift.

The Lottery (Yust, 1969, 18 minutes)

A faithful adaptation of the famous and allegorical Shirley Jackson short story, *The Lottery* is a significant title in the educational film canon. It has a simple visual style and was shot on location with a cast that includes local nonprofessionals. The story concerns a community lottery whose tragic purpose is unknown, although there are signs it will be ominous, including that each of the neighbors collects at least one large stone as they make their way to the lottery assembly, and one especially nervous woman's resistance to the fairness of the process. When the single winner is selected, the twist ending reveals that her "prize" is being stoned to death by her neighbors, both children and adults, which takes place offscreen.

The Man Without a Head/L'Homme Sans Tête (Solanas, 2003, 18 minutes)

A Jury Prize winner at Cannes, *The Man* is a French short from Argentinean director Juan Solanas that uses live-action and computer-generated imagery to tell a surreal story about the protagonist, Mr. Phelps, a young man with romance on his mind but no head. After making a date with a young woman to attend a ball, Mr. Phelps makes elaborate preparations that mostly involve his attempt to buy a head at a specialty shop. He finds that none of the available heads are appropriate to his needs and personality, so he arrives for his date in his natural state, much to the apparent delight of the young woman. *The Man* is a light comedy with a touch of the musical, as Mr. Phelps dances delightedly in preparation for the ball; it is also fanciful and upbeat, despite its mostly dreary industrial setting, which is rendered in beautiful, epic-scale wide shots.

Me The Terrible (Decker, 2012, 11 minutes)

Me the Terrible is an art short and adventure tale whose fanciful sensibility and plucky protagonist recall *The Red Balloon* and *Two Men and a Wardrobe*. It tells the story of a pirate girl with heroic intentions who sails alone, except for her teddy bear, to New York City, where she plans to conquer its landmarks; but her journey ends in disappointment. *Me*'s inventive, exuberant scenario and visuals combine archival footage, a quick rhythm, and playful special effects to capture the girl's triumphs and her dispiriting encounter with meanness, especially the theft of her beloved bear. In the end, she returns to her boat alone, with a broken heart, and on the verge of an uncertain future.

Megatron (Crisan, 2008, 14 minutes)

A Palme d'Or winner, *Megatron* is a deeply moving and understated Romanian art short about the long journey a single mother and her son take to the city for his eighth birthday to visit MacDonalds, where the boy also expects to meet his father. Shot in a naturalistic style using long-duration shots, the film is attentive to conveying the distance between the mother and son's home and their city destination, which speaks also to the challenges of their relationship. As they travel, the awful tension between them deepens when the already-sullen, frustrated boy learns his mother has not invited the father, whom she implies is uninterested in seeing the son. Eventually she permits the boy to call his father, and he hangs up believing he'll arrive. But like the "megatron" of the title, a promotional action figure the boy wants and MacDonalds has run out of, it seems unlikely that the father will fulfill his son's birthday wish.

Mumbler/Mompelaar (Roels and Reygaert, 2007, 22 minutes)

A low-key Belgian horror art short and winner of a jury award at Clermont-Ferrand, *Mompelaar* tells an odd, unsettling, and enigmatic story, which evokes the sensibilities of both John Waters and David Lynch. Its protagonist is an awkward young man who mumbles rather than speaks and lives in the country with his "mother"—who is clearly played by a transvestite with a five o'clock shadow, wig, and dress. The mood becomes very dark when the man finds a dead body in a forest clearing, and bloody clothes nearby seem to suggest more victims, including a small child. Thereafter the plot is convoluted and baffling, though it seems the mumbler is a murderer who collects things for and from his victims. In the end, to the delight of his mother, he brings home a group of tourists, whose guide he has decapitated after what might have been a sexual exchange between the two, which reveals the mumbler's tail! The mumbler has very bad intentions, as he proceeds to poison the group of tourists. In the end, many questions remain unanswered though there are a few twisted possibilities: Is this a fairy tale with a monster, the mumbler, who is a kind of Pied Piper to the tourists, and perhaps more victims? Or is his "mother" the monster who controls the mumbler's strings?

New Boy (Green, 2007, 12 minutes)

Based on a short story by Roddy Doyle, *New Boy* is an allegorical Irish art short that tells the moving and earnest yet unsentimental story of the titular protagonist who arrives at an apparently all-white school after suffering a horrible tragedy in an unnamed African country. With a fairly complex organization, *New Boy* shifts between the present, in the Irish school, and the past, at the school in his native country where his kind, dedicated teacher was murdered by state soldiers. As the new boy in school, he finds himself tormented by the class bullies at recess, but he fights back. While he and the bullies are waiting to be disciplined by the teacher, the new boy makes a joke by quietly mocking the teacher's tendency to begin her sentences with the word "now," which elicits the bullies' laughter and the beginning of a new friendship. *New Boy*'s representation of the boy's present and past is unified by the shared school settings, which are contrasted by means of overexposed imagery in the present day and saturated-color sequences from the past.

The New Tenants (Back, 2009, 21 minutes)

An Academy Award winner, *The New Tenants* is a dark and eccentric comedy about a gay couple thrilled to be moving into a New York City apartment. Unfortunately, they quickly learn that the apartment's previous tenant was murdered and has left much drama in his wake, including an elderly neighbor who needs flour for a baking project, an angry husband who's convinced his wife is cheating on him, and a drug dealer who thinks his big stash of heroine is in the apartment because it was stolen by the murdered guy. Things spin further out of control and reach murderous proportions, until the couple simply waltzes out of the apartment and the film ends with them gracefully dancing on a bridge.

An Occurrence at Owl Creek Bridge
(Enrico, 1962, 27 minutes)

A legendary short, *Occurrence* won the Palme d'Or at Cannes and an Academy Award. Adapted from the Ambrose Bierce short story, *Occurrence* is a longer short that is fascinating for its play with character subjectivity conveyed via point-of-view shots, a legendary twist ending, and the use of space to convey the passage of time. During the American Civil War, a prisoner is hung for tampering with a bridge, but he manages to escape and sets out on the long journey home. Visual contrasts suggest the difference between reality, conveyed more naturalistically, and the man's interiority, conveyed via stylized imagery—especially slow-motion and freewheeling mobile camera work. Although it uses dialogue very sparingly, a song is used to indicate what the doomed man is thinking and feeling.

One Too Many/Éramos Pocos (Cobeaga, 2006, 16 minutes)

A dark comedy with a twist that was nominated for an Academy Award, *One Too Many* begins in medias res as a woman is leaving an apartment in a hurry. It turns out she's a wife and mother who's finally fed up with her lazy, slovenly, television-addicted husband and young adult son. When the father takes his son to collect their grandmother at the nursing home, so that she can take the place of the missing wife, she is only too pleased to oblige. A clever use of montage and careful comic secrets and revelations economically and amusingly convey the benefits she brings to the undeserving but thankful pair, including her excellent housekeeping and cooking skills. But, after the apartment is entirely tidied and their bellies are full of delicious food, the father begins to suspect she isn't really their grandmother after all. When the father gets suspicious, he calls his wife and looks through the family photographs until he realizes his houseguest is really a stranger. A second twist follows that unexpected revelation as the father decides to keep his discovery to himself.

The Old Woman's Step/No Passo da Véia
(Malaquias, 2002, 15 minutes)

A Brazilian short with a dry sense of humor about a sly and diligent old woman who endures several hardships when she goes to the village market to sell her chicken in order to buy a gift of deodorant for her lovely, young fisherman grandson. After presenting him with his gift, she convinces her grandson to take a shower, which he does outside. As she sits in the background of a carefully composed deep-space and deep-focus wide shot while gazing at her showering grandson's wet, shiny, backlighted body positioned in the foreground, it becomes clear that the old woman has cleverly orchestrated the complex series of steps in order to reach this perfect (and a bit perverse) moment of visual pleasure.

La Perra (Maza, 2004, 16 minutes)

A Chilean art film, *La Perra* is a darkly humorous tale about a decadent, vulgar, self-absorbed and economically privileged couple whose amorous inclinations are apparently enabled when they project their malevolent impulses onto their new maid, whom they repeatedly refer to as "the bitch." As the quiet, respectful country servant diligently performs her duties, her vicious employers expect (or hope) she'll steal them blind. Frustrated to no end, the couple enacts the nasty business of planting a money lure to prove themselves right but the maid doesn't bite, which angers the wife even more. Her response to the maid's honesty is to fire her and give her the cash, whereupon she tells her husband the maid stole the money and fled, leaving them to fend for themselves in their messy house.

Pourvu Qu'on Ait L'Ivresse . . . (Pollet, 1958, 20 minutes)

The winner of the Golden Lion Award for Short Film at the Venice Film Festival, *Pourvu* (whose title roughly translates as "Provided They Are Drunk . . .") was much beloved by directors associated with the French New Wave, including Jean-Luc Godard. A French art film with a spare story, it is also a compelling documentary-fiction hybrid, whose only setting is a large dance hall, and whose soundtrack consists of nonsynchronous music from the dance hall's band. The protagonist is a shy young man who spends hours, from daylight until late into the night, people-watching and hoping to enlist a dance partner. The hall's dancers are celebratory and enthusiastic, and more so as the day progresses, and fascinating as they represent a diverse array of shapes, sizes, races, ethnicities, ages, and dancing styles and abilities. The young man is not only bashful but less than handsome, and when he finally musters the courage to ask one potential partner for a dance, her refusal is heartbreaking. Finally, after a wedding party arrives, the young man bolsters his resolve with a silly costume nose, mustache, and hat and gets his one and only dance partner—a bride, and he seems to have fun even if his dancing skills are not topnotch. In the end, the young man seems to assess himself in the mirror before going off, apparently to try his luck again.

Ray's Male Heterosexual Dance Hall
(Gordon, 1987, 23 minutes)

An Academy Award winner, *Ray's* is a comedy that satirizes the kind of masculine privilege and entitlement nurtured in homosocial members-only settings. When the recently unemployed protagonist discovers that there's a place where executives schmooze during lunch hour, he jumps at the chance to go. But, instead of a new job, he finds a strictly observed hierarchy and set of rules made more stifling by the crowded claustrophobic space and sea of nearly indistinguishable dark suits, ties, and white shirts. Besides mocking the absurdities of some masculine rituals, *Ray's* also conveys the desperation of workers at the mercy of systems and rules that are opaque to them. In addition, *Ray's* is indicative of visually conservative but sometimes bold shorts made during the 1980s, with running times suited for television.

Robbie (Harvey, 2012, 9 minutes)

An Australian science-fiction short, *Robbie* is fascinating for using existing footage only, primarily from NASA, in conjunction with the protagonist's first-person narration. Robbie is a sentient robot who's been stuck alone on a space station for decades and whose life span is nearly complete. Although he's an optimist and recounts happy memories, especially of the times he shared with long-ago human colleagues, Robbie's situation and loneliness are remarkably sad and seemingly never-ending.

Sexy Thing (Pentecost, 2006, 14 minutes)

An Australian art short that played in competition at Cannes, its protagonist is Georgie, a just-adolescent tomboy who's infatuated with her best girlfriend and with the ocean and its sea life. The opening images of Georgie swimming while gracefully turning and floating, and all alone, are both beautiful and suggestive of her character, as she has painful secrets about her father's sexual abuse that alienate her from her family and, perhaps, her best friend. *Sexy Thing* is organized nonchronologically and uses dialogue very sparingly, and the characterization of Georgie is mostly visual, but it has considerable depth—especially the moments that convey her subjectivity when she imagines she's safe swimming in the water.

The Sheep Thief (Kapadia, 1997, 24 minutes)

An art drama and student short that played in competition at Cannes, *The Sheep Thief* is the tale of a lonely young Indian orphan boy who is introduced as he steals a sheep and is caught and branded on the forehead to mark him as a thief. Using a scarf as a headband to hide his shame, the boy finds his way to a family that takes him in and he joins them as they pick and sell the beautiful mangoes from what looks like an ancient tree. The family's small sons are enchanted by the boy who entertains them with tricks that convince them he has magical powers. The thief's idyll is broken when the local villagers demand that the family exile him because he's undertaken an elaborate ruse by stealing some precious religious artifacts and blaming someone else, so that he could "find" the objects and be embraced as a hero. *Thief* uses a naturalistic visual style and a pattern of point-of-view shots that enable identification with the boy who, like the protagonist of the Italian Neorealist classic *The Bicycle Thieves*, is on the bottom rung of the social and economic ladder, with few resources for survival.

Short & Curlies (Leigh, 1987, 18 minutes)

A art short with a fairly complex, episodic story, *Curlies* is a dry comedy that combines humor and pathos in its offbeat and entirely engaging study of three principle characters, a young woman who's a pharmacy clerk, Joy; the awkward jokester, Clive, who woos her; and the nervous, breathless beautician, Betty, who repeatedly transforms the clerk's hair and chats with her about the details of her life, which contrast very much with her own sullen daughter's. Clive's primary character trait is his penchant for odd and less-than-amusing wordplay, which he uses to seduce and eventually become engaged to Joy. The film ends on Joy's wedding day, while she's getting her hair done yet again, much to the delight of Betty, and much to the chagrin of Betty's hopeless daughter.

So You Want to Be a Detective (Bare, 1948, 11 minutes)

One of the long-running Joe McDoakes comedy series titles, *Detective* is an amusing Warner's Vitaphone parody of the hard-boiled detective genre that borrows situations from classic noir titles like *The Maltese Falcon* and *Dark*

Passage (with the latter's point-of-view camera). *Detective*'s plot is twisty, and its over-the-top protagonist, Phillip Snarlow, is given to talking back to the voiceover narrator. The visual gags are plentiful, including a dead woman in a file cabinet, a mysterious "Tall Man"—on stilts—and a pile of dead men that fall out of an impossibly small wardrobe one-by-one, like dominos. The ending also provides a twist, as it turns out that Joe McDoakes has only been dreaming he's Snarlow, after falling asleep during his janitorial duties at the real detective's desk.

Star in the Night (Siegel, 1945, 22 minutes)

A classic short from Hollywood's studio era, *Star* was Don Siegel's directorial debut and the Academy Award winner for Best Two Reel Short. With an unadorned set-bound visual style, it nevertheless stands out for the strong performances from its ensemble cast. A sentimental retelling of the Nativity story for modern times, it begins on Christmas Eve with three cowboys on horseback who are (inexplicably) loaded down with gifts and decide to head for a bright star they spot in the distance. When they reach the star, it turns out to be part of a motel sign, which the grumpy Italian proprietor is in the midst of installing. The hitchhiker who stops to chat has a big heart and tries to explain the spirit of Christmas to the proprietor, who's having none of it as he's fed up with the selfish, unkind, and demanding patrons at his inn. But when a young couple arrives and there isn't a room for them, a few of the women usher the wife to a shed where they discover she's going to have a baby, which the other travelers soon learn too. Not surprisingly, all of the previously nasty customers become kindly and solicitous, and things end happily—and with great earnestness—as the motel keeper tearfully ponders an image of the nativity.

Tanghi Argentini (Thys, 2006, 14 minutes)

A Belgian comedy with a dry sensibility and a flair for physical humor, *Tanghi* was nominated for an Academy Award and won several festival awards including at Clermont-Ferrand. The protagonist is Andres, a chubby office worker who delights in giving Christmas gifts to his colleagues that he's carefully tailored to their individual needs and desires. When Andres asks a rather stern senior colleague, Frans, to give him tango lessons to impress a woman he fancies, Frans and Andres make a great coach–student team and practice at every opportunity including, hilariously, when they pass each other in the hall at work. When coach and student go to the dance hall so Andres can seduce his dream woman with his new skills, there's a twist as it turns out Andres has been scheming to get Frans and the woman together all along, as his Christmas gift to Frans.

Terry Tate: Office Linebacker (Thurber, 2003, 4 minutes)

A fast-paced and over-the-top comedy short, *Terry* has a very rudimentary narrative about the titular football player and office manager who has a fierce commitment to office rules. Each time a co-worker breaks one of the rules, even a minor one, he immediately sets things right by tackling the offender with great vigor, despite some exaggerated disparities in size, power, and gender between Tate and his victims.

The Tonto Woman (Barber, 2007, 36 minutes)

The Tonto Woman is a Western art short with a longer, more complex narrative adapted from a short story by Elmore Leonard that was nominated for an Academy Award. With lush cinematography and framings that recall *The Searchers* (Ford, 1956), *Woman* has a measured pace and compelling structure, with most of the story told in flashback. It tells a captive narrative tale about a married woman who has been kidnapped by Apaches shortly after her wedding and enslaved for eleven years. When her wealthy cattle baron husband rescues her, he banishes her to a shack on his desert property so that her "shame"—a facial tattoo given to her by her captors—will be out of sight. Despite her isolation, a dashing cattle thief comes upon her while she's bathing and becomes fascinated by her. The attraction is mutual and the thief manages to draw her out of her exile and into her own identity; but when he takes her into town for an excursion, her shame is fully on view, and her husband arrives to make his claim for his wife.

Traffic/Trafic (Mitulescu, 2004, 15 minutes)

A Romanian art short that won the Palme d'Or, *Traffic* is a darkly enigmatic portrait of an unexceptional but prosperous-looking businessman on his meandering way to a meeting. His most remarkable characteristic is his apparent detachment from others, which is underscored by his steady demeanor, and by the pattern of tight telephoto shots and awkward claustrophobic framings that isolate him from others, even on busy streets. During his slow journey, he stops in a parking lot to visit his daughter, but only for a few moments; an angry co-worker arrives at his car to collect something, and he has a series of cryptic one-sided cell-phone conversations. Although there is a slim narrative thread that concerns the possibility that his daughter swallowed something dangerous, he remains remote though it seems to be a symptom of modern urban life, as suggested by his odd and also brief conversation with a stranger—a young street vendor woman—who seems perhaps more removed than he is.

Trevor (Rajski, 1994, 17 minutes)

An over-the-top comedy-musical art short and Academy Award co-winner, Trevor's charming protagonist is crazy about Diana Ross, convinced he should devote his life to the theater, and both enjoys and is troubled by his early adolescent attraction to boys—especially cute Pinky, a local baseball star. Trevor, who shares his diary entries and thoughts in direct address and voiceover narration, is also preoccupied with suicide. In an opening montage that recalls Harold and Maude (1971), he's introduced in a series of death poses (including, hilariously, one that recreates the famous painting, "The Death of Marat"), while his unruffled parents go about their business. When the kids accuse him of acting gay and Pinky rejects him, Trevor decides to commit aspirin suicide while listening to Ross's "Endless Love," which lands him in the hospital but on the way to a fabulous ending, owing to a cute candy striper boy.

United We Stand/De beste går først
(Moland, 2002, 9 minutes)

A deeply dry comedy art short from Norway, United We Stand's simple story involves a group of elderly soldiers embarking on their annual hike while earnestly singing a song of solidarity. As the men leave for their camp in the woods, they begin to sing a protest song until they hear a woman calling for help in the distance. They soon find her but she's stuck in a bog and steadily sinking. The men move into heroic action and pull the woman to safety, only to realize they are all now stuck in the bog. An amusing series of shots shows the straight line of men as they sink lower and lower, and at the same rate, though their moods don't seem to change. To make the most of a bad situation, the men sing the Soviet song "The Internationale," which calls workers to arise from their "slumbers." The irony, of course, is that there will be no more arising for these old soldiers.

Victoria Para Chino (Fukunaga, 2004, 13 minutes)

A student film, *Victoria Para Chino* is a searing social issue drama that won several international festival awards. Based on a true story with a tragic outcome, *Victoria* concerns a group of ninety Mexican immigrants, adults, and children who board an apparently refrigerated truck bound for Houston, Texas. Soon after they depart, things begin to go badly as bits of light reveal several faces drenched with sweat and fear, especially a father with his toddler. Despite their efforts to get more air by punching through the truck's wall and to get the driver's attention, the immigrants remain trapped. When the non-Spanish speaking driver finally stops and opens the trailer, several bodies fall out, both alive and dead; however, instead of summoning help, the driver walks away. In the end, as the epilogue reveals, nineteen immigrants perished in the truck, which was found abandoned in the desert town of Victoria. The story's raw power is enhanced by beautiful cinematography that contrasts the gold-tinged wide-open vistas of the desert with the dark, claustrophobic, terrifying interior of the truck.

Wind/Szél (Iványi, 1996, 7 minutes)

A Hungarian art short that won the Palme d'Or at Cannes, *Wind* is based on a still photograph, Lucien Hervé's "The Three Women." Consisting entirely of one very slow, long-duration circular pan shot, without dialogue, it begins in medias res as a trio of three middle-aged women are shown standing in front of a house in a rural landscape while looking off-screen. Tension develops when the camera pans in the opposite direction of their gazes, and finally reveals what they see: a harrowing scenario in which a group of men have been or are being executed by hanging. The ending is open as nothing is revealed about the women, the executed men, or their executioners.

The Youth in Us (Leonard, 2005, 12 minutes)

An earnest, sentimental story about a teenage couple who seem to be on the verge of having sex for the first time, when the long-withheld establishing shot reveals a twist—they are in a hospital where the girl is apparently dying. The confusion about the couple's intentions continues as the girl asks the boy to tell her the story about the "first time he did it." The story is enacted in flashback, and concerns the time the boy happened upon an injured, suffering, and dying deer that he euthanized. The film's intense ending is the result of the surprise revelation that the boy, in an act of love, apparently intends to put his dying girlfriend out of her misery too.

Zapping (Mungiu, 2000, 15 minutes)

A Romanian art short with a darkly absurd and surreal sensibility, Zapping is about a working-class man who seems to spend hours in his apartment watching television by zapping from one station to the next. He continues switching channels until he lands on a program that shows a couple having sex, and he's startled when the male partner stops to talk to and taunt the viewer. The sex man explains that he too used to be a constant zapper but was punished by being made to function as a remote control. Seems the unnamed authorities have confined a collection of men to hospital beds where they are on twenty-four-hour call to shift channels by "turning the wheel," which evokes the worker-eating machine in Metropolis. When the remote guy tells the zapper to do something else, "play football, read a book," the police arrive to intervene—as it seems that's the worst thing a remote can say, and the worst thing a television watcher can do.

Notes

1 Introduction

1. Bell, "Eat My Shorts."
2. Cooper and Dancyger, *Writing the Short Film*, 4.
3. Scott, "An Oscar Film Festival."
4. Raskin, *Art of the Short Fiction Film*, 1.
5. Raskin also founded the journal *Short Film Studies* in 2011. Each issue is devoted to analyses of two or three titles, which are announced in advance for potential contributors.
6. Staiger, "Politics of Film Canons," 9.
7. See Sarris, *The American Cinema*, 16–27.
8. Ibid., 20.
9. Rehrauer, *The Short Film*, 1.
10. Beairsto, *The Tyranny of Story*, 9.
11. Thurlow, *Making Short Films*, 9.
12. Raskin, *Art of the Short Fiction Film*. The strategy is also used in the journal *Short Film Studies*, which Raskin founded.
13. According to my count, of the 625 titles on the registry (as of the last round of selections in 2013), thirty-nine are live-action fiction shorts, which is about 6 percent; of the sound era titles, there are sixteen, which is about 2.5 percent. See http://loc.gov/film/registry_titles.php
14. See Lund, "What's a Short Film, Really?" 106; and Wolf, "What Is Cinema."
15. Bell, "Eat My Shorts."
16. Beairsto, *The Tyranny of Story*, 11.
17. Yeatman, "What Makes a Short Fiction Film Good?," 154.
18. Nash, *Short Films*, 51.
19. Ibid., 7.
20. Douieb, "More Than a Stepping Stone."
21. See the Program Guide at: http://telluridefilmfestival.org/show/program_ guide

22. See Knafo, "Bringing 'Where the Wild Things Are.'"

23. McLaughlin, "Short Sighted," 62.

24. Cooper and Dancyger, *Writing the Short Film*, 3. It's also worth noting that the only English-language academic books that focus on the general category of the live-action fiction short are both written by European authors, Richard Raskin in Denmark and Symon Quy (whose volume is addressed to secondary school teachers) in England.

25. Quoted in Badal, *Swimming Upstream*, 98.

26. Knight and Porter, *A Long Look at Short Films*, 6.

27. Thoreau, "Letter to Mr. B: Harrison Blake," 375–376.

28. Reinker, *Minutenkino*, 5.

29. Thurlow, *Making Short Films*, 2.

30. Scott, "An Oscar Film Festival."

31. Quoted in Phillips, *Writing Short Scripts*, xi.

32. Phillips, *Film*, 258.

33. Knight and Porter, *A Long Look at Short Films*, 8.

34. Beairsto, *Tyranny of Story*, 12.

35. Munroe, *How Not to Make a Short Film*, 29.

36. Cooper and Dancyger, *Writing the Short Film*, 1.

37. Raskin, *Art of the Short Fiction Film*, 3. Raskin's characterization of the "true" short fiction film reflects his preference for complex and interpretively open films, which the present volume includes in the "art short" category.

38. Lund, "What's a Short Film, Really?" 108.

39. See http://www.filmsshort.com/short-short-films/#.VFRGheeTa3w and http://www.shortoftheweek.com/tag/micro/

40. Raskin, *Art of the Short Fiction Film*, 3. For a discussion of the German term "novelle," see Pasco, "On Defining Short Stories," 123. For the French term "nouvelle," see Cortázar, "Some Aspects of the Short Story," 246.

41. Wolf, "What is Cinema," 1–2.

42. Quy, *Teaching Short Films*, 10.

43. Italics in original; Diffrient, 11.

44. Ibid.

45. Italics in original; Ibid., 4.

46. Ibid., 209.

47. Orgeron, et. al., *Learning With the Lights Off*.

48. Woolf, "Modern Fiction," 288. Also quoted in Quy, *Teaching Short Films*, Worksheet 13, 1.

49. Sarris, *The American Cinema*, 27, 19.

2 Shorts and Film History: The Rise, Fall, and Rise of the Short Film

1. Beairsto, *The Tyranny of Story*, 11.
2. Nash, *Short Films*, 13–14.
3. Staiger, "Hollywood Mode of Production," 128–134.
4. Thompson, "Formulation of the Classical Style," 171; Quinn, "Distribution," 37–39.
5. Staiger, "Blueprints for Feature Films," 187–188; Staiger, "Hollywood Mode of Production," 128–132.
6. Staiger, "Hollywood Mode of Production," 100, 129; Quinn, "Distribution," 35.
7. Staiger, "Blueprints for Feature Films," 180; Quinn, "Distribution," 47.
8. Thompson, "Formulation of the Classical Style," 179; Bradley, *First Hollywood Sound Shorts*, 19.
9. Koszarski, *An Evening's Entertainment*, 164.
10. Maltin, *Great Movie Shorts*, 1.
11. Gomery, *Hollywood Studio System*, 19; Gomery, *Shared Pleasures*, 77.
12. Koszarski, *An Evening's Entertainment*, 48.
13. Levy, "Shorts No Longer Just 'Fillers,'" 28.
14. Crafton, *The Talkies*, 381; Koszarski, *An Evening's Entertainment*, 163–164.
15. Maltin, *Great Movie Shorts*, 1–2.
16. Crafton, *The Talkies*, 88.
17. King, "Introduction: Beyond Vitaphone," 247–248; Crafton, *The Talkies*, 85, 88.
18. Crafton, *The Talkies*, 93, 101, 252, 381.
19. Maltin, *Great Movie Shorts*, 192; King, "Introduction: Beyond Vitaphone," 247. King clarifies such disregard by arguing that the early sound shorts reflected a deepening division between two comedy traditions—the more highly valued "sophisticated humor," which was associated with dialogue-based comedy popular in metropolitan theaters, and the "sensationalism of 'low' comedy," associated with action-oriented slapstick exaggerated with noisy sound effects, which was popular in small towns; see King, "The Spice of the Program," 319–322.
20. Bradley, *First Hollywood Sound Shorts*, 120.
21. Gomery, *Hollywood Studio System*, 24.
22. King, "Introduction: Beyond Vitaphone," 249.

23. Crafton, *The Talkies*, 386.

24. Bradley, *First Hollywood Sound Shorts*, 120.

25. Gomery, *Hollywood Studio System*, 71–72.

26. For a discussion of serial shorts, which construct "very long and complex screen narratives" and are thus different than series-based shorts that do not depend upon a chronological screening order, see Koszarski, *An Evening's Entertainment*, 164–170.

27. Bradley, *First Hollywood Sound Shorts*, 19.

28. Quimby, "Short Subjects Developing Ground," 25.

29. Gomery, *Hollywood Studio System*, 4, 45, 97.

30. Okuda and Watz, *Columbia Comedy Shorts*, 1–2.

31. Bradley, *The First Hollywood Sound Shorts*, 128.

32. Ibid.; King, "The Spice of the Program," 319–322.

33. Diamond, "Paramount," 30.

34. See Schatz, *Old Hollywood*, 169–171.

35. Gomery, *Hollywood Studio System*, 171, 121.

36. Knight and Porter, *A Long Look*, 55–56.

37. Fulton, "A University Course," 201.

38. Petrie, "Theory, Practice," 31.

39. Ibid., 37; also see Schatz, *Old Hollywood*, 203–204.

40. Levy, *Cinema of Outsiders*, 35.

41. Schatz, *Old Hollywood*, 203–204; Petrie, "Theory, Practice," 38; Levy, *Cinema of Outsiders*, 35.

42. "The Student Movie Makers," 80–82.

43. Burgess, "Student Film-Making," 29.

44. See oscars.org/awards/saa/history.html

45. Fensch, *Films on the Campus*, 19–22.

46. Ibid., 31, 76.

47. Ibid., 52–56.

48. Ibid., 65, 211–212.

49. Shatnoff, "Report from New York," 73.

50. See "Third National Student Film Festival"; "The Student Movie Makers."

51. Weinraub, "If You Don't Show Violence."

52. Polanski, *Roman*, 123.

53. Higham, "Polanski." Also see, Weinraub, "If You Don't Show Violence"; and Alvarez, "Can Polanski Make a Star of Polanski?"

54. Maltin, *Great Movie Shorts*, viii.

55. Adler, "Don't Sell Shorts Short," 1D.
56. Fehrenbach, *Cinema*, 232. It was founded as the West German Educational Film Festival; in 1959, it was renamed the West German Short Film Festival; and in 1991, it was given its current name, the International Short Film Festival Oberhausen.
57. Cowie, *Revolution*, 119.
58. Fehrenbach, *Cinema*, 223–225.
59. Ibid., 218–219.
60. Polanski, *Roman*, 149.
61. See www.kurzfilmtage.de/ and http://www.clermont-filmfest.com/index.php?m=274
62. See Tropfest.com
63. Horak, "Archiving," 114.
64. Alexander, *Films You Saw*, 8.
65. See http://www.sho.com/sho/short-stories
66. Katz, "Atom Seeking Shorts."
67. AtomFilms was purchased by MTV in 2006 (see Zeitchik, "Short Attention Span"); it was folded into Comedy Central in 2007 (see Keegan, "Online Comedy Business Booming").
68. Munroe, *How Not to Make a Short Film*, xiv.
69. Adams, "Short Shrift No Longer."
70. Davies, "Long History of Short Film."

3 Short Film Specificity: Narrative Compression, Unity, Character, and Endings

1. Godard, "Take Your Own Tours," 109.
2. Ofield, "Regarding Short Film Promotion."
3. Lewis, *How to Make Great Short Feature Films*, 12.
4. Thompson, *Formulation of the Classical Style*, 163–173.
5. Adler, "Don't Sell Shorts Short," D11.
6. Emphasis in original; Bordwell and Thompson, *Film Art*, 70–71; Thompson, "Formulation of the Classical Style," 167–168.
7. Quoted in Pratt, "Short Story," 94.
8. Poe, "Poe on Short Fiction," xv.
9. Ibid., 60, 61, 63.
10. Quoted in March-Russell, *Short Story*, 33.

11. Poe, "Poe on Short Fiction," 61.
12. Chekhov, "Short Story," 197.
13. Quoted in Pratt, "Short Story," 101.
14. Ibid.
15. For Poe, see March-Russell, *Short Story*, 165; for May's, Lukács's, and Harris's views, see May, *The Short Story*, 20, 116, and 13–14 respectively.
16. Ramsay, "Lynne Ramsay Interview."
17. Eisenstein, "Short Fiction Scenario," 9.
18. Ibid., 22. Eisenstein made his presentation soon after Germany's invasion of the Soviet Union in order to propose that the film industry concentrate its resources on making short fiction films to rally citizens during the crisis.
19. Eisenstein, "Short Fiction Scenario," 10.
20. Cooper and Dancyger, *Writing the Short Film*, 226; Quy, *Teaching Short Films*, 10.
21. Evans, "Rushes," 5.
22. Thompson, "Formulation of the Classical Style," 168.
23. Phillips, *Film: An Introduction*, 258.
24. Quy, Worksheet 10.
25. March-Russell, *Short Story*, 120.
26. Eisenstein, *Short Fiction Scenario*, 15.
27. Raskin, *Art of the Short Fiction Film*, 95.
28. March-Russell, *Short Story*, 121.
29. Cooper and Dancyger, *Writing the Short Film*, 131.
30. Nash, *Short Films*, 91. Likewise, Phillips emphasizes that the short film protagonist's personality does not change; see *Film*, 259.
31. *The Lonely Voice*, 19. Also see March-Russell for his observation that in the short story there is a "predisposition towards outsiders"; *Short Story*, 122.
32. O'Connor, *The Lonely Voice*, 17. See also story theorist Charles E. May who echoes O'Connor in saying the "short story's shortness has traditionally been closely related to a sense of loneliness and alienation"; *Short Story*, 117.
33. Bordwell, *Narration in the Fiction Film*, 157–159.
34. Thompson, "Formulation of the Classical Style," 176.
35. Quoted in Pratt, "Short Story," 98.
36. Ibid., 99.

37. Cooper and Dancyger, *Writing the Short Film*, 9.
38. *Most*'s story corresponds with the tale of the "drawbridge keeper," a well-known urban legend that turns on the father's moral crisis. The Tobias Wolff short story "The Night in Question" also uses the legend.
39. May, *Short Story*, 57.
40. Ibid., 61, 67.
41. Nash, *Short Films*, 83.
42. Thurlow, *Making Short Films*, 15.
43. May, *Short Story*, 116.
44. Éjxenbaum, "O. Henry," 81–82.
45. Eisenstein, *Short Fiction Scenario*, 31.
46. Nash, *Short Films*, 89. In literature, the twist ending is most often associated with O. Henry's short stories and the use of ironic patterns in the service of narrative closure and intensity; see May, *Short Story*, 44.
47. See Bordwell, *Narration in the Fiction Film*, 55.
48. Eisenstein, *Short Fiction Scenario*, 32.
49. Quoted in Munroe, *How Not to Make a Short Film*, 36.
50. Ramsay, "Lynne Ramsay Interview."

4 Storytelling and Style: The Classical Short

1. Bordwell et al., *Classical Hollywood Cinema*, 157–193; Bordwell and Thompson, *Film Art*, 94–96.
2. Beairsto, *Tyranny of Story*, 16.
3. Rohrberger, "Between Shadow and Act," 43.
4. Emphasis in original; Gunning, "Cinema of Attraction," 65–66.
5. Gunning, "Crazy Machines," 93.
6. Tom Gunning cites the closely related Hale's Tours theaters that showed films made from moving vehicles; see Gunning, "Cinema of Attraction," 65.
7. Geoff Alexander explains that *Rendezvous*' speed was accelerated to produce the effect of faster motion; see Alexander, *Films You Saw in School*, 217.
8. Gunning, "Cinema of Attraction," 66.
9. Gunning, "Crazy Machines," 95.
10. Ibid., 80.
11. Ibid., 88–90.
12. Ibid., 91.

13. Karnick and Jenkins, *Classical Hollywood Comedy*, 67, 358n12.
14. Staiger, "Blueprints for Feature Films," 175.
15. Branigan, "Towards a Pragmatics of Narrative," 24.
16. "Of Local Origin," *New York Times*.
17. Joe Amodei, quoted in Badal, *Swimming Upstream*, 64–65.
18. *Confection* is one of Saks's "New York Trilogy" of shorts, each of which was inspired by the events of 9/11; the other two titles are *Colorforms* (2003) and *Date* (2004).
19. Lund, "What's a Short Film," 109.
20. March-Russell, *Short Story*, 32–41.
21. In addition to its Academy Award, *Six Shooter* won Best British Short at the British Independent Film Awards and Best Short at the Irish Film Awards.
22. James, "Martin McDonagh."
23. Carroll, "Martin McDonagh's *The Pillowman*," 180.
24. Botvinick, "Bloodied Light."
25. Badal, *Swimming Upstream*, 59.
26. See Krutnik, "A Spanner in the Works?" 19.
27. Crafton, *The Talkies*, 386.
28. Bradley, *First Hollywood Sound Shorts*, 126.
29. For a discussion of parodies and their exploitation of the "already formulated narrative framework," see Krutnik, "A Spanner in the Works?" 19.

5   Storytelling and Style: The Art Short

1. Williams, *Republic of Images*, 217–218; also see Hodsdon, "*Zéro de conduite*."
2. Nowell-Smith, *Making Waves*, 3, 13.
3. Ibid., 74.
4. Ibid., 17, 34–35, 71–78, 122, 108–109.
5. Ibid., 105.
6. Vincendeau, "Introduction," 138.
7. Koresky, "The Red Balloon."
8. Gibson, "What Childhood Films"; Gleiberman, "Hope Floats"; and Koresky, "The Red Balloon."
9. Rafferty, "Two Short Fables."
10. Williams, *Republic of Images*, 310.

11. Lamorisse had worked as a documentary filmmaker prior to making his fiction shorts *White Mane* (1953) and *The Red Balloon*, as was also the case for a few of the filmmakers associated with the French New Wave, including Alain Resnais.

12. Gleiberman, "Hope Floats."

13. Gibson, "What Childhood Films."

14. Koresky, "The Red Balloon."

15. Gibson, "What Childhood Films."

16. An entirely dialogue-free version of *The Red Balloon* was widely distributed on the 16mm non-theatrical circuit in the United States.

17. The effect was the result of thin wires attached to the balloon—actually a series of identical red balloons, which were controlled by off-screen wranglers to create the illusion of independent movement.

18. Rafferty, "Two Short Fables."

19. Gleiberman, "Hope Floats."

20. Bazin, "The Virtues and Limitations of Montage," 41–46.

21. Hohenadel, "Paris for Real"; Rafferty, "Two Short Fables." Also, in my short film class, students have offered several readings of the ending, including that it is "scary," "happy," and "good revenge" on Pascal's bullies.

22. Solomons, "The Up-lifting Inspiration for Pixar."

23. Quoted in Itzkoff, "ARTSBEAT."

24. Adams, "Bought for TV," 71.

25. Koresky, "The Red Balloon." *The Red Balloon*'s continuing legacy includes the short and feature-length films that have paid homage to or parodied it including the Taiwanese filmmaker Hou Hsaio-Hsien's 2007 feature *The Flight of the Red Balloon* and the short animated parodies *Dream Doll* (Godfrey and Grgic, 1979) and *Billy's Balloon* (Hertzfeldt, 1998). There was also a musical stage adaptation, written by Anthony Clark, performed at the Royal National Theatre in London in 1996 and in New York City in 2000. See Clark and Lamorisse, "*The Red Balloon*." Finally, it was restored and rereleased by the prestigious distributor Janus/Criterion in 2008.

26. Koresky, "The Red Balloon."

27. *Two Men* won several festival awards, including the Bronze Medal for Experimental Film at the 1958 Brussels World's Fair; honorable mention at Oberhausen; and the Golden Gate Award at the San Francisco International Film Festival.

28. Geuens, *Film Production Theory*, 49. Also see Geuens, 49–51, for his discussion of *Two Men* as a text that exemplifies Martin Heidegger's conception of art as something that depicts a familiar world in a profoundly
unfamiliar way in order to reveal a significant "Truth." In the case of *Two
Men*, Geuens argues that it provides the realization "that the society into
which we fit so well has a dark side after all, and that we are more likely
in our everyday life to behave like the . . . thugs . . . than the innocent
wanderers who came from the sea."

29. Delahaye and Narboni, "Interview with Roman Polanski," 30; Polanski,
"Script," 3.

30. Raskin, *Art of the Short Fiction Film*, 30.

31. In addition to Chabrol's screenplay, his apartment was also a location,
and Rivette's friends Jean-Claude Brialy and Doniol-Valcroze were principal actors; see Neupart, *A History of the French New Wave*, 165. The
careful viewer will also spot several *Cahiers du Cinema* critics playing
extras during the party scene, including Chabrol, Godard, and Truffaut.

32. MacCabe, *Godard*, 142.

33. Holmes and Ingram, *Francois Truffaut*, 3. Throughout their volume,
Holmes and Ingram return to *Les Mistons* for its use of themes, characters, and other strategies that Truffaut would return to during his career.

34. Bernhardt, "*Les Mistons*," 52.

35. Alan Williams notes that *Les Mistons* was originally twenty-seven-
minutes long; the currently available version is an abridged one re-edited
by Truffaut. See *Republic of Images*, 426 n10.

36. Dixon, "*Les Mistons*"; Kael, "The Mischief-Makers," 388.

37. Bernhardt, "*Les Mistons*," 52–53.

38. Neupert, *A History*, 172.

39. Holmes and Ingram, *Francois Truffaut*, 39.

40. For his extensive discussion of *Les Mistons*, which includes information
about its production history, a nuanced narrative analysis, and finely
detailed attention to its cinematography, see Neupert, *A History*,
165–177.

41. *Charlotte et Véronique* is also known as *Tous les Garçons S'Appellent
Patrick*/*All Boys are Called Patrick*.

42. MacCabe, *Godard*, 97.

43. Now outlawed, the Cracker Night event was a much-beloved tradition
when families and neighbors in Australia got together to set off fireworks.

44. Crimmings, "A Documentary after the Fact," 6.

45. For a more in-depth analysis of *Skaterdater* and its historical and cultural significance, see Felando, "*Skaterdater: Short Film, Long Ride*," 51–55.

46. Available on http://twocarsonenight.com/

47. Pasco, "On Defining Short Stories," 125.

48. Quoted in Raskin, "An Interview with Mitko Panov." For in-depth discussions, analyses, and additional material related to *Wind*, see Raskin, *Art of the Short Fiction Film*, which devotes a full chapter to the film.

49. Gordimer, "The Flash of Fireflies," 264.

50. *Wasp* won scores of awards, including an Oscar and the top prize at the Oberhausen festival in Germany.

51. Brody, "Does the Cinema Need Short Films?"

Bibliography

Adams, Sam. "Short Shrift No Longer." *Los Angeles Times* (February 10, 2008): http://articles.latimes.com/2008/feb/10/entertainment/ca-shorts10

Adams, Val. "'The Red Balloon' is Bought for TV." *The New York Times* (October 25, 1960): 71.

Adler, Renata. "Don't Sell Shorts Short." *The New York Times* (April 28, 1968): D1, 11.

Alexander, Geoff. *Films You Saw in School: A Critical Review of 1,153 Classroom Educational Films (1958–1985) in 74 Subject Categories.* Jefferson: McFarland & Company, 2014.

Alvarez, A. "Can Polanski Make a Star of Polanski?" *The New York Times* (February 22, 1976): http://timesmachine.nytimes.com/timesmachine/1976/02/22/122819492.html

Badal, Sharon. *Swimming Upstream: A Lifesaving Guide to Short Film Distribution.* Amsterdam: Focal Press, 2008.

Bazin, Andre. "The Virtues and Limitations of Montage." In *What is Cinema? Volume I*, edited by Hugh Gray, 41–52. Berkeley: University of California Press, 1967.

Beairsto, Ric. *The Tyranny of Story: Audience Expectations and the Short Screenplay.* Vancouver: Vancouver Film School, 1998.

Bell, J. "Eat My Shorts." *Sight and Sound* (May 2004): www.bfi.org.uk/sightandsound/feature/237

Bernhardt, William. "*Les Mistons* [Review]." *Film Quarterly* 13(1) (Autumn 1959): 52–53.

Bordwell, David. *Narration in the Fiction Film.* Madison: The University of Wisconsin Press, 2008.

Bordwell, David, and Kristin Thompson. *Film Art: An Introduction.* New York: McGraw-Hill, 2012.

Bordwell, David, Janet Staiger, and Kristin Thompson. *The Classical Hollywood Cinema: Film Style & Mode of Production to 1960.* New York: Columbia University Press, 1985.

Botvinick, Marshall. "Bloodied Light: The Cinema of Martin McDonagh."
    Film International (May 25, 2011): http://filmint.nu/?p=2082

Bradley, Edwin M. *The First Hollywood Sound Shorts, 1926–1931*. Jefferson:
    McFarland & Company, 2009.

Branigan, Edward. "Towards a Pragmatics of Narrative." In *Towards a
    Pragmatics of the Audiovisual: Volume II: Theory and History*, edited by
    Jürgen E. Müller, 1–38. Munster: Nodus Publications, 1995.

Brody, Richard. "Does the Cinema Need Short Films?" *The New Yorker*
    (March 18, 2014): http://www.newyorker.com/search?q=does+the+cine
    ma+need+short+films%3F

Burgess, Jackson. "Student Film-Making: First Report." *Film Quarterly* 19(3)
    (Spring 1966): 29–33.

Carroll, Noël. "Martin McDonagh's *The Pillowman*, or the Justification of
    Literature." *Philosophy and Literature* 35(1) (April 2011): 168–181.

Chekhov, Anton. "The Short Story." In *The New Short Story Theories*, edited
    by Charles E. May, 195–198. Athens: Ohio University Press, 1994.

Clark, Anthony, and Albert Lamorisse. *The Red Balloon* [Stage Adaptation].
    London: Oberon Books, 1999.

Cooper, Pat, and Ken Dancyger. *Writing the Short Film*. Burlington: Elsevier
    Focal Press, 2005.

Cortázar, Julio. "Some Aspects of the Short Story." In *The New Short Story
    Theories*, edited by Charles E. May, 245–255. Athens: Ohio University
    Press, 1994.

Cowie, Peter. *Revolution: The Explosion of World Cinema in the Sixties*.
    New York: Faber and Faber, 2004.

Crafton, Donald. *The Talkies: American Cinema's Transition to Sound,
    1926–1931*. New York: Charles Scribner's Sons, 1997.

Crimmings, Emma. "A Documentary After the Fact." In *Short Site: Recent
    Australian Short Film*, edited by Emma Crimmings and Rhys Graham,
    3–6. Victoria: Australian Centre for the Moving Image, 2004.

Davies, Rebecca. "The Long History of Short Film." *The Telegraph* (April 18,
    2010): http://www.telegraph.co.uk/culture/film/film-life/7593291/The-
    long-history-of-short-films.html

Delahaye, Michel, and Jean Narboni. "Interview with Roman Polanski." In
    Roman Polanski: Interviews, edited by Paul Cronin, 13–30. Jackson:
    University of Mississippi Press, 2005.

Diamond, Lou. "Paramount Has Its Exchanges Check Box Office Before
    Making Plans." *The Film Daily* (April 28, 1936): 30.

Diffrient, David Scott. *Omnibus Films: Theorizing Transauthorial Cinema.* Edinburgh: Edinburgh University Press, 2014.

Dixon, Wheeler Winston. *"Les Mistons."* *Senses of Cinema* 38 (February 2006): http://sensesofcinema.com/2006/cteq/mistons/

Douieb, Corin. "More Than a Stepping Stone: BAFTA Shorts 2013." *Aesthetica* (April 1, 2013): http://www.aestheticamagazine.com/bafta-shorts-2013

Eisenstein, Sergei. *On the Composition of the Short Fiction Scenario.* Calcutta: Seagull Books and Eisenstein Cine Club, 1984.

Éjxenbaum, B. M. "O. Henry and the Theory of the Short Story." In *The New Short Story Theories*, edited by Charles E. May, 81–88. Athens: Ohio University Press, 1994.

Evans, Gareth. "Rushes: Oberhausen Notes: Shorts Circuit." *Sight and Sound* 12(7) (July 2002): 5.

Fehrenbach, Heide. *Cinema in Democratizing Germany: Reconstructing National Identity After Hitler.* Chapel Hill: The University of North Carolina Press, 1995.

Felando, Cynthia. *"Skaterdater:* Short Film, Long Ride." *CineAction* 94 (2014): 51–55.

Fensch, Thomas. *Films on the Campus.* South Brunswick: A. S. Barnes and Company, 1970.

Fulton, A. R. "A University Course in the Moving Pictures." *Hollywood Quarterly* 3(2) (Winter 1947–1948): 199–201.

Geuens, Jean-Pierre. *Film Production Theory.* Albany: State University of New York Press, 2000.

Gibson, Brian. "What Childhood Films Are These?" *Vueweekly.com* (December 12, 2007): http://www.vueweekly.com/what_childhood_films_are_these/

Gleiberman, Owen. "Hope Floats." *Entertainment Weekly* (November 21, 2007): www.ew.com/ew/article/0,,20162166,00.html

Godard, Jean-Luc. "Take Your Own Tours." In *Godard on Godard: Critical Writings by Jean-Luc Godard*, edited by Jean Narboni and Tom Milne, 107–116. New York: Viking Press, 1972.

Gomery, Douglas. *Hollywood Studio System.* New York: St. Martin's Press, 1986.

Gomery, Douglas. *Shared Pleasures: A History of Movie Presentation in the United States.* Madison: University of Wisconsin Press, 1992.

Gordimer, Nadine. "The Flash of Fireflies." In *The New Short Story Theories*, edited by Charles E. May, 264. Athens: Ohio University Press, 1994.

Gunning, Tom. "The Cinema of Attraction: Early Film, Its Spectator and the Avant-Garde." *Wide Angle* 3(4) (1986): 64–70.

Gunning, Tom. "Crazy Machines in the Garden of Forking Paths: Mischief Gags and the Origins of American Film Comedy." In *Classical Hollywood Comedy*, edited by Kristine Brunovska Karnick and Henry Jenkins, 87–105. New York: Routledge, 1995.

Higham, Charles. "Polanski: 'Rosemary's Baby' and After." *The New York Times* (September 23, 1973): http://timesmachine.nytimes.com/timesmachine/1973/09/23/97455930.html

Hodsdon, Bruce. "*Zéro de conduite.*" *Senses of Cinema* (December 2013): http://sensesofcinema.com/2013/cteq/zero-de-conduite/

Hohenadel, Kristin. "Paris for Real vs. Paris on Film: We'll Always Have the Movies." *The New York Times* (November 25, 2001): http://www.nytimes.com/2001/11/25/movies/film-paris-for-real-vs-paris-on-film-we-ll-always-have-the-movies.html?module=Search&mabReward=relbias%3As%2C{%221%22%3A%22RI%3A5%22}

Holmes, Diana, and Robert Ingram. *François Truffaut.* Manchester: Manchester University Press, 1998.

Horak, Jan-Christopher. "Archiving, Preserving, Screening 16mm." *Cinema Journal* 45(3) (Spring 2006): 112–118.

Itzkoff, Dave. "ARTSBEAT; A Time Burton Cloud for Macy's Sunny Skies." *The New York Times* (October 22, 2011): http://query.nytimes.com/gst/fullpage.html?res=9900E6D8103BF931A15753C1A9679D8B63&module=Search&mabReward=relbias%3Ar%2C{%221%22%3A%22RI%3A7%22}

James, Caryn. "Martin McDonagh Finds His Inner Thug as Film Director." *The New York Times* (April 4, 2006): http://www.nytimes.com/2006/04/04/movies/04jame.html?module=Search&mabReward=relbias%3As%2C{%221%22%3A%22RI%3A5%22}

Kael, Pauline. "*The Mischief-Makers* (*Les Mistons*)." In *Kiss Kiss Bang Bang*, 388–389. New York: Bantam Books, 1968.

Karnick, Kristine Brunovska, and Henry Jenkins. "Introduction: Funny Stories." In *Classical Hollywood Comedy*, edited by Kristine Brunovska Karnick and Henry Jenkins, 63–86. New York: Routledge, 1995.

Katz, Richard. "Atom Seeking Shorts: New Distribbery Banks on 'Net.'" *Variety* (February 28, 1999): https://variety.com/1999/film/news/atom-seeking-shorts-1117491764/

Keegan, Terence. "Online Comedy Business Booming." *Variety* (November 12, 2007): http://variety.com/2007/digital/news/online-comedy-business-booming-1117975892/

King, Rob. "Introduction: Beyond Vitaphone: The Early Sound Short." *Film History* 23(3) (2011a): 247–250.

King, Rob. "'The Spice of the Program': Educational Pictures, Early Sound Slapstick, and the Small-Town Audience." *Film History* 23(3) (2011b): 313–330.

Knafo, Safi. "Bringing 'Where the Wild Things Are' to the Screen." *The New York Times* (September 2, 2009): http://www.nytimes.com/2009/09/06/magazine/06jonze-t.html?pagewanted=all

Knight, Derrick, and Vincent Porter. *A Long Look at Short Films; An A.C.T.T. Report on the Short Entertainment and Factual Film.* Association of Cinematograph, Television, and Allied Technicians in Association with Pergamon Press, 1967.

Koresky, Michael. "The Red Balloon." http://www.criterion.com/current/posts/655-the-red-balloon, date of publication: April 28, 2008.

Koszarski, Richard. *An Evening's Entertainment: The Age of the Silent Feature Picture, 1915–1928.* Berkeley: University of California Press, 1994.

Krutnik, Frank. "A Spanner in the Works? Genre, Narrative and the Hollywood Comedian." In *Classical Hollywood Comedy*, edited by Kristine Brunovska Karnick and Henry Jenkins, 17–38. New York: Routledge, 1995.

Levy, Emanuel. *Cinema of Outsiders: The Rise of American Independent Film.* New York: New York University Press, 2001.

Levy, Jules. "Shorts No Longer Just 'Fillers'; Must Be Vital Factor at Box Office." *The Film Daily* (April 28, 1936): 28.

Lewis, Ian. *How to Make Great Short Feature Films: The Making of "Ghosthunter."* Oxford: Focal Press, 2001.

Lund, Andrew. "What's a Short Film, Really?" In *Swimming Upstream: A Lifesaving Guide to Short Film Distribution*, edited by Sharon Badal, 106–112. Amsterdam: Focal Press, 2008.

MacCabe, Colin. *Godard.* New York: Farrar, Straus and Giroux, 2003.

Maltin, Leonard. *The Great Movie Shorts: Those Wonderful One- and Two-Reelers of the Thirties and Forties.* New York: Bonanza Books, 1967.

March-Russell, Paul. *The Short Story: An Introduction.* Edinburgh: Edinburgh University Press, 2009.

May, Charles E. *The Short Story: The Reality of Artifice.* New York: Routledge, 2002.

McLaughlin, Noel. "Short Sighted: Short Filmmaking in Britain." *Cineaste* 26(4) (2001): 62–63.

Munroe, Roberta. *How Not to Make a Short Film: Secrets from a Sundance Programmer.* New York: Hyperion Books, 2009.

Nash, Patrick. *Short Films: Writing the Screenplay.* Harpenden: Kamera Books, 2012.

Neupert, Richard. *A History of the French New Wave Cinema.* Madison: The University of Wisconsin Press, 2007.

Nowell-Smith, Geoffrey. *Making Waves: New Cinemas of the 1960s.* New York: Bloomsbury Academic, 2013.

O'Connor, Frank. *The Lonely Voice: A Study of the Short Story.* New York: Harper Colophon Books, 1985.

"Of Local Origin." *The New York Times* (October 5, 1945): http://timesmachine. nytimes.com/timesmachine/1945/10/05/88303447.html

Ofield, Jack. "Regarding Short Film Promotion." *The Short List* (January 25, 2002): www.shortfilm.de/index.php?id=897&L=2&print=1

Okuda, Ted, and Edward Watz. *The Columbia Comedy Shorts: Two-Reel Hollywood Film Comedies, 1933–1958.* Jefferson: McFarland & Company, 1986.

Orgeron, Devin, Marsha Orgeron, and Dan Streible (eds.). *Learning With the Lights Off: Educational Film in the United States.* Oxford: Oxford University Press, 2011.

Pasco, Allan H. "On Defining Short Stories." In *The New Short Story Theories*, edited by Charles Edward May, 114–130. Athens: Ohio University Press, 1994.

Petrie, Duncan. "Theory, Practice, and the Significance of Film Schools." *Scandia* 76(2): 31–46.

Phillips, William H. *Writing Short Scripts.* Syracuse: Syracuse University Press, 1991.

Phillips, William H. *Film: An Introduction.* Boston: Bedford/St. Martins, 2009.

Poe, Edgar Allan. "Poe on Short Fiction." In *The New Short Story Theories*, edited by Charles E. May, 59–72. Athens, OH: Ohio University Press, 1994.

Polanski, Roman. *Roman.* New York: William Morrow and Company, 1984.

Polanski, Roman. "Script." In *Roman Polanski: Interviews*, edited by Paul Cronin, 3–7. Jackson: University of Mississippi Press, 2005.

Pratt, Mary Louise. "The Short Story: The Long and the Short of It." In *The New Short Story Theories*, edited by Charles E. May, 91–113. Athens, OH: Ohio University Press, 1994.

Quimby, Fred. "Short Subjects Developing Ground for New Talent Needed By Studios." *The Film Daily* (April 28, 1936): 25.

Quinn, Michael. "Distribution, the Transient Audience, and the Transition to the Feature Film." *Cinema Journal* 40(2) (Winter 2001): 35–56.

Quy, Symon. *Teaching Short Films.* London: BFI, 2007.

Rafferty, Terrence. "Two Short Fables That Revel in Freedom." *The New York Times* (November 11, 2007): http://www.nytimes.com/2007/11/11/movies/11raff.html?pagewanted=all&module=Search&mabReward=relbias%3As%2C{%221%22%3A%22RI%3A9%22}&_r=0

Ramsay, Lynne. "Lynne Ramsay Interview." *Ratcatcher*, DVD. Directed by Lynne Ramsay. New York City: Janus/Criterion, 2002.

Raskin, Richard. *The Art of the Short Fiction Film: A Shot by Shot Study of Nine Modern Classics.* Jefferson: McFarland & Company, 2002.

Raskin, Richard. "An Interview with Mitko Panov on *With Raised Hands.*" *P.O.V.: A Danish Journal of Film Studies* 15 (March 2003): http://pov.imv.au.dk/Issue_15/section_1/artc3A.html

Rehrauer, George. *The Short Film: An Evaluative Selection of 500 Recommended Films.* New York: Macmillan Information, 1975.

Reinker, Susanne. *Minutenkino = Minute-Movies.* Munich: Goethe Institute, 1991.

Rohrberger, Mary. "Between Shadow and Act: Where Do We Go from Here?" In *Short Story: Theory at a Crossroads*, edited by Susan Lohafer and Jo Ellyn Clarey, 32–45. Baton Rouge: Louisiana State University Press, 1989.

Sarris, Andrew. *The American Cinema: Directors and Directions 1929–1968.* Chicago: University of Chicago Press, 1968.

Schatz, Thomas. *Old Hollywood/New Hollywood: Ritual, Art, and Industry.* Ann Arbor: UMI Research Press, 1983.

Scott, A. O. "An Oscar Film Festival, All in One Screening." *The New York Times* (February 10, 2011): http://www.nytimes.com/2011/02/11/movies/11oscar.html?pagewanted=all

Shatnoff, Judith. "Report from New York." *Film Quarterly* 20(4) (Summer 1967): 73–76.

Solomons, Gabriel. "The Uplifting Inspiration for Pixar." *Vueweekly.com* (December 12, 2007): www.vueweekly.com/article.php?id=7536

Staiger, Janet. "Blueprints for Feature Films: Hollywood's Continuity Scripts." In *The American Film Industry*, edited by Tino Balio, 173–194. Madison: The University of Wisconsin Press, 1985a.

Staiger, Janet. "The Hollywood Mode of Production to 1930." In *The Classical Hollywood Cinema: Film Style & Mode of Production to 1960*, edited by

David Bordwell, Janet Staiger, and Kristin Thompson, 85–154. New York: Columbia University Press, 1985b.

Staiger, Janet. "The Politics of Film Canons." *Cinema Journal* 24(3) (Spring 1985): 4–23.

"The Student Movie Makers." *Time* 91(5) (February 2, 1968): 80–82.

"Third National Student Film Festival Sponsored by MPAA, Four $500 Grants." *Rochester Institute of Technology Reporter* 42(11) (January 19, 1968): 4.

Thompson, Kristin. "The Formulation of the Classical Style, 1909–28." In *The Classical Hollywood Cinema: Film Style & Mode of Production to 1960*, edited by David Bordwell, Janet Staiger, and Kristin Thompson, 155–240. New York: Columbia University Press, 1985.

Thoreau, Henry David. "Letter to Mr. B: Harrison Blake, November 16, 1857." In *Familiar Letters of Henry David Thoreau*, edited by F. B. Sanborn, 371–378. Boston: Houghton, Mifflin, 1894.

Thurlow, Clifford. *Making Short Films: The Complete Guide from Script to Screen*. Oxford: Berg, 2005.

Vincendeau, Ginette. "Introduction: IN FOCUS: The French New Wave at Fifty: Pushing the Boundaries." *Cinema Journal* 49(4) (Summer 2010): 135–138.

Weinraub, Bernard. "'If You Don't Show Violence the Way It is,' says Roman Polanski, 'I Think That's Immoral and Harmful. If You Don't Upset People Then That's Obscenity'; A Visit with Roman Polansky." *The New York Times* (December 12, 1971): http://timesmachine.nytimes.com/timesmachine/1971/12/12/91315926.html?pageNumber=112

Williams, Alan. *Republic of Images: A History of French Filmmaking*. Cambridge: Harvard University Press, 1992.

Wolf, R. W. "What is Cinema – What is Short Film?" *shortfilm.de* (2006): www.shortfilm.de/index.php?id=2645&L=2&print=1

Woolf, Virginia. "Modern Fiction." In *The Virginia Woolf Reader*, edited by Mitchell A. Leaska, 283–291. San Diego: Harcourt Brace Jovanovich, 1984.

Yeatman, Bevin. "What Makes a Short Fiction Film Good?" *P.O.V.: A Danish Journal of Film Studies* 5 (1998): 151–162.

Zeitchik, Steven. "Short Attention Span: Media Players Take Big Look at Mini-Movies." *Variety* (November 5, 2006): http://variety.com/2006/film/news/short-attention-span-1117953265/

Index

Printed and bound in the United States of America